Ha Will Travel

Equestrian Adventuresses Book Four

KRYSTAL KELLY

COPYRIGHT INFORMATION

Equestrian Adventuresses Book 4: Have Breeches Will Travel

Copyright © 2020 by Krystal Kelly.

All characters and names in this book have been changed for privacy protection.

Copyright © Equestrian Adventuresses 2020. All Rights Reserved.

For all the adventuresses not afraid to put on their big girl breeches...
You will see the world.

Table of Contents

Vampires, Werewolves & Jackals in Romania 13

Desert to the Atlantic..........................39

Adventures in Sicily..........................78

Tales of an Equine Vet in the Kalahari Desert 112

Randolph County 138

Icebergs & Icelandic Horses in Greenland....164

Preface
Welcome to the Equestrian Adventuresses Tribe!

Thank you for being a part of this wonderful adventure. Putting together a collection of stories from women who speak a variety of languages and have traveled far and wide on horseback hasn't been easy. We've featured women's amazing true stories throughout this series, including adventuresses from Poland, Belgium, Australia, the USA, the UK, New Zealand, Germany and many others. Their inspiring stories have taken us to places such as Georgia, India, Mongolia, Italy, Canada, South Africa, Namibia, Romania, Greenland, Chile, Argentina and Bhutan.

In no other equestrian book series has so many international readers and riders come together in one place and I am very excited to say that because of these stories young girls in Yemen, India, and others can be taken to far-away places on horseback and be inspired and encouraged to follow their dreams.

Having spent more than a decade working with horses in male-dominated countries where women are not allowed to ride, this book series has been a dream come true for me. When I was a little girl, unable to afford riding lessons or a horse of my own, I would lose myself in books and stories of girls riding horses and having adventures. I told myself that one day I would be surrounded by horses and it was because of books like these that fueled my ambitions into one day turning into a reality.

These pages contain true stories. Many of the authors do not speak English as a first language. Although we did our best to edit the stories and translate their words, a few minor mistakes here and there are expected for a big project and undertaking such as this. But the stories are what counts and these women didn't hold back! They bravely take us to unexplored lands, trail blaze new paths and journey across exotic destinations, all from atop a horse.

I hope you enjoy each and everyone of their stories as much as I have and remember to share this book with as many of your friends and future adventuresses as possible! You never know which story might spark the hidden flame that enables someone's life to change forever. I hope these tales empower future girls and women around the globe to saddle up, head for the horizon and see where they end up.

"My heart belongs to the arena but my soul belongs to the trail." -Anonymous

Yours Truly,
Krystal Kelly

Founder of Equestrian Adventuresses
www.EquestrianAdventuresses.com

DOWNLOAD YOUR FREE TRAVEL GUIDE FOR EQUESTRIANS E-BOOKS TODAY!

www.EquestrianAdventuresses.com

In this Book Series you will find:
- Stables Listings of Horse Riding Tour Operators in the USA and Worldwide
- Information and travel tips for a variety of countries including sights to see, highlights not to miss and much more
- Resources to plan your ideal horse riding vacation based on your budget, riding level/discipline, time of year, terrain, accommodation and weather preferences
- 70+ Job Ideas on how to work internationally with horses
- Tips and tools how you can work abroad with horses as a volunteer or as a paid position and career

And much, much more!

To find our free e-books simply visit:
www.EquestrianAdventuresses.com

Vampires, Werewolves & Jackals in Romania

BY KRYSTAL KELLY

I sit in the chair unnerved as the young woman in front of me applies the glue to my upper lip that will allow the mustache to stick. I crinkle my nose as she applies the hairs to my once bare face as I adjust to the feeling. Being a female my entire life, I never quite imagined I'd be sitting behind the set of an American Hollywood Film—in Transylvania, Romania no less!—wearing a man's wardrobe.

And it had to be prostitute day. Always, without fail. It seemed every time I got to play a movie stuntwoman...it was prostitute day. (Which was ironic considering this was my first time to be in a Hollywood movie.) All the female extras scurried around the makeup and wardrobe as they dawned their fishnet stockings, high heel shoes, painted on red lipstick and curly-cues...while I was the only woman on set to dawn a mustache.

Needless to say, I was determined to work it. Especially considering the gorgeous, blue-eyed, tall, dark, and handsome film crew guy that prepared the set while eyeing me non-stop. We exchanged various smiles and giggles from across the room as I stood in full attire to admire myself.

"Wow...I'm not going to lie to you," I said to my male admirer, "I'm the best-looking man here!" I winked before returning outside to tend to my horse—the real star of the movie as far as I was concerned.

Of course, the British and American actors in the movie agreed with me completely. I mounted my horse and waited for my cue from the Director with the others as the celebrities joked with me. "You're just jealous because they needed to add me to the movie because there weren't enough good-looking men with mustaches in this film..." I smiled as the two gorgeous male actors threw back their heads in laughter. Both of them had mustaches, neither of which had been superglued to their faces.

"Just be sure you don't steal focus..." The British actor flashed me a smile.

I shrugged as I gathered my reins to prepare for the shot. The adorable film crew guy, who had decided to not only bring me a cup of tea earlier that cold winter morning but also felt the need to sing to me in French, and flashed me a thumbs-up as I waited for my cue. Everything seemed easy enough so far. Little did I know that lunchtime later that day would have me scrambling to eat my meal without getting food caught in my mustache. (Much harder than it looks.)

I sighed heavily as I looked up towards the sky. I couldn't believe the irony of the situation. After all, I was an American living in a small village in Romania, on the set of a Hollywood Horror film—about Werewolves—during the full moon, only days away from Halloween.

Talk about being in the right place at the right time! I think to myself and focus on the task at hand: to not let my mustache get in the way of flirting with the cute, blue-eyed film crew guy.

****

The sun had only just come up when I arrived in Romania. During my time working in Belgium, I had the pleasure to make friends with a thirty-year-old woman from Romania. She had invited me into her country and home to stay with her and although I never fully understood at the time whether it was out of politeness or genuine friendliness, she seemed just as excited as I to be reunited again after almost one year apart.

Although I was fatigued from the long flight, I found myself alert and excited. After all, I had never been to Romania before, and although I was technically homeless and jobless, as far as I was concerned I was simply on a vacation in Romania until the time a job could be found—wherever it may be.

The Romanian people fascinated me. Women were wearing old-fashioned clothes, long skirts, scarves on their heads, and shoes as I could only imagine having been worn by Amish people in the States. The men too had a different look to them, though having just come from Egypt to me it was much more Westernized. I found my seat on the bus and simply listened to the Romanian language being tossed back and forth. It was a pleasant language.

At this particular point in my life, I was so accustomed to speaking in Arabic that I found myself even thinking in Egyptian. A few of the words in Romanian sounded very similar to me in my second language and I wondered if it had something to do with the Persian influence on the country many hundreds of years ago.

A smile crossed my lips as I gazed out the window at the beautiful green landscape and countryside—something that I had not seen during my stay in Egypt. Despite the ache in my chest and the lack of sleep and utter exhaustion at all the unknown possibilities for my life (*would I find a job, where would I go, how long will I stay in Romania, what will happen to all my friends in Egypt?*) I felt a calm wash over me. Something told me that despite all the doors that had recently been slammed on my face, there were countless new doors that had been opened. I knew that there was a reason I had come to Romania. I could feel it in my bones. I was meant to be here.

Though what that reason was...I had yet to discover.

Alina was waiting for me when my bus arrived. After I had left the job in Belgium, Alina worked there for a total of six months before returning home to Romania. After her return, she found herself unable to find work. Although she had survived working for an Olympic rider for six months, it seemed no equestrian stables in Romania was ready to hire her due to her lack of equestrian experience. Until my second day in the country, that is, when she got a phone call from one of the stables.

"A week ago," she explained to me, "I had a job interview at a stable not too far from here in a nearby village. The owner of the stables had turned me down at the time and told me that he wouldn't hire me, but today he called me again because apparently, he is having an overload of customers this weekend and he wants me to come and help. I told him that I'm having a friend from America with me who is a horse trainer that worked with me in Belgium and so as soon as I mentioned this he told me to bring you along with me. We will stay there for the whole weekend if you don't mind. He is having a room for us both and we will be eating our meals there with him and the customers." She flashed me a pleading look before adding, "I know you're on vacation and you wanted to go exploring tomorrow but I've been wanting to work for him for a very long time and I'm hoping that if I go there and prove myself over the weekend that he will hire me."

I smiled a big smile, "Of course I don't mind! I'm happy to come and eat and sleep and ride some horses around for free while you do all the work." I winked playfully.

I arrived at the stables in a very good mood. Alina had gone ahead earlier that morning while I had enjoyed the day with her older brother and his girlfriend in the nearby town of Sighisoara. It was such a beautiful place. The village was built inside a Citadel and the castle walls, though thousands of years old, still looked majestic. The cobblestone streets and the picturesque cafes and restaurants had my heart aflutter. It was almost as if you could breathe the history in the air and I savored every minute of it. I had also had my very first encounter with Dracula himself as the very café we ate our lunch was none other than Vladimir Dracul's birthplace and childhood home. Vladimir is the reason behind the many legends and stories which inspired the original book, *Dracula* by Bram Stoker.

Vlad Dracula, or "Vlad the Impaler" as he's also known, was a Romanian King back in the 1400s and is a national treasure to the locals. Vlad's reputation for his cruelty among his enemies during the many battles he fought in his lifetime was the inspiration for the vampire stories we know today. Romania has a history of legends about the "strigoi" (what we call vampires) and to the local people, Vlad the Impaler was a hero, having fought against the Ottomans, Strigoi, and countless other evil spirits. He kept the Romanian people free during his reign and is still today considered one of the most important people in their history.

I waved goodbye to Alina's brother and girlfriend as they drove away, leaving me and my suitcase alone in the countryside. I looked up at the large guesthouse where all the customers slept and ate their meals. I took one final deep breath as I walked inside to find the owner of the stables and Alina.

The inside of the guesthouse was even more charming than it was from the outside. I smiled softly as I looked outside the large glass windows from floor to ceiling overlooking the rolling hills and horses in the fields. The large wooden table took up the entire dining room and I struggled to count how many people could be seated at once.

"Krystal?" A man catches my eyes and flashes me a peculiar look. I nod my head "yes" as I look him up and down.

"Are you Ionut?" I ventured a guess, unsure of how to properly pronounce the name belonging to the Owner of the stables.

"Yup that's me!" He shook my hand. "You're late," he said.

"I'm late?" I crinkled my nose and brow as I thought to myself, *but I'm on vacation!*

"That's right, you're late. Go put your bag in the room and get out to the barn to help the customers unsaddle their horses. We are winding up for the day and dinner will be inside here in an hour." He motioned for me to follow him as he led me outside to my room. Alina and I were to be sharing a room similar to the ones the customers were given. I wasted no time and simply placed my bags on the empty bed before wandering outside in search of the "customers."

That night at the dinner table, I felt myself being interviewed by Ionut. "How many years have you worked with horses, where have you worked before, what kind of horses have you worked with," these were the sort of questions being launched at me as I shoveled my dinner into my mouth.

"I've worked in several states in the USA. I'm a certified horse trainer and show jumping rider. I've also recently worked in Belgium for a 5 time Olympic Eventing rider, and I just came here from Egypt where I worked in Cairo the past year for an FEI Level II Showjumping Coach and world-class rider." I answered, trying to be short and to the point. I was on holiday after all and hadn't planned on discussing horses.

Ionut grinned. "Tomorrow morning you'll ride out with us. I have something special for you to ride with me first thing in the morning before the customers wake up." He flashed me a smile and I knew instantly that this "special horse" was a test.

I shrugged. I was used to being "tested" with green, half-wild horses. This seemed to be a common practice in the equestrian industry. I'd developed a "velcro butt" over the years and was mostly unfazed by these sneaky attempts at assessing my ability as a rider.

"Does this 'special horse' have a name?" I ask.
"The Jackal."

The next morning, bright and early, I sat atop the Jackal with Ionut standing in the center of the arena. It was too early for any of the customers to be awake, and even my friend Alina was still in bed. *So much for my vacation...* I thought.

As much as I silently tried to protest, truth be told, I was intrigued. I was curious about the Jackal and eager to see what he would do. Ionut didn't say a word as I began warming him up around the arena. The Jackal was a big beautiful, bay warmblood. He carried his head proudly in the air and the second I set foot in the stirrups he was eager to move.

He launched himself forward into strong, powerful gaits. He didn't just walk, trot or canter, he WALKED, TROTTED, and CANTERED. This horse meant business. I could only describe his canter stride as "mini rears." His front legs struck high in the air with every step as he rocked onto his haunches, launching himself forward in a powerful canter stride that would certainly scare the breeches off a "normal rider."

In my career thus far, I had ridden a few Olympic horses. Their movements felt HUGE, even when the horses themselves were considered "small." (A 16hh warmblood is considered small, as most can tower to about 18 or even 19 hands.) That is how I felt when I sat atop the Jackal.

I started to laugh. I so enjoyed this horse's mighty canter strides that I found myself not wanting him to end it. Luckily for me, he wasn't ready to end it anytime soon so I simply sat back and rode it, allowing him to canter until his heart's content. I didn't try to contain or stop it, I simply "directed it," really making him work. I'd found that the best way to deal with high energy horses was to keep them busy and make them perform more interesting tasks such as canter leg yields, flying changes, half pass, and things of the like. After all, I wanted to see what this horse could do, so why not test all the buttons and see which ones were installed?

Ionut remained silent throughout, observing me carefully. My laughter took him aback and I could have sworn I saw him trying to hide a smile.

I eventually slowed the Jackal down and began to cool him off. The horse let out a big sigh of relief as if he too had enjoyed being able to blow off some steam without being fought with or "controlled."

I walked towards Ionut, a big smile on my face. "He's lovely!" I patted his beautiful, strong neck.

"Good, you'll ride him again this morning during our trail ride with the customers. No one has been able to ride him out on a trail before so you'll ride in the front so I can be between you and the customers just in case he decides to take off."

I dismounted and gathered the reins to lead him back to the stables. "Ok. He hasn't been ridden on a trail before?" I asked, surprised. This was a trail riding stables for tourists, after all. It seemed strange to me to have a horse in the stables which couldn't perform the only job required at the yard.

"No. Before today, he hadn't been ridden for two years because until today no one else could handle him."

My eyebrows shot up at the news. A part of me was proud of my accomplishments, but another part of me was angry that he was only just now telling me this. *What would have happened if I wasn't as good of a rider as you thought I was?!* I wanted to shout. I knew for some reason it's perfectly normal to put a rider's life at risk by asking them to ride crazy horses, as I had done for years, but at what point would I stop and realize that risking my life or hospital visits in foreign countries wasn't worth it?

Obviously, not today.

I rolled my eyes, accepting my fate, and accepting this as a very real necessity when working with horses. *It comes with the job,* I told myself.

That day I enjoyed a nice long ride across the Romanian countryside. And I did it atop one of the most fun horses I had ridden in a long time. The Jackal had power, energy, spunk, and pep in his step. Although his power walk was too much for the customer's horses, I managed to complete the entire 2-hour ride without any mishaps or tribulations.

I felt proud of myself and proud of this beautiful, misunderstood horse at the end of our ride. After helping the customers to put away their horses, Ionut caught me as I was making my way to the dinner table.

"Krystaldo!" Ionut blurted, "You're hired."

"I'm hired?" I thought aloud. I didn't even know what I was being hired for.

****

It was absolutely pouring rain. In America you always hear the expression, "raining cats and dogs," but as I spurred my horse through the thick trees in the Transylvanian forest in the country of Romania all I could think was "it's raining vampires and gypsies!" Not that I'd seen a vampire yet. It was only my first month working and living in this country with horses and since one of my favorite trail rides overlooked the small villages and the "Gypsy housing development" as my boss loved to tell the tourists, the only thing I thought I hadn't seen yet was the famous Dracula himself.

But right now, Dracula was the furthest thing from my mind. After all, today was a big day for me. I had already been working at the stables for a few weeks but had yet to take the tourist customers out on one of our three-hour-long trail rides without the company of my boss. But today was my day. Mind you, I only had one other girl with me and she was a fellow Romanian citizen who frequented the stables on her weekend getaways from the busy city life and to escape the mundane existence of her job away from horses and gypsies and country living, but she was a customer none the less. And I was in charge of leading her out on a trail ride. Just me. All by myself. Oh, and did I mention that it was raining?

Nothing before this moment in my life had ever seemed to faze me or worry me. Not when I moved to Cairo, Egypt on the day the country erupted into turmoil as it revolted against its leader. Nor was I worried when I was warned to avoid the large dogs in Romania with big sticks on their necks as these were known as the vicious shepherd dogs guarding the sheep so severely they had been known to kill unfortunate people wandering the hillside alone.

But I was worried now. After all, I was riding down a trail I had only ridden once before when I had first taken the job in Romania. And I had been riding the trail from the other direction...oh yeah and it hadn't been raining vampires and gypsies.

Careful not to panic my only trail companion-slash-valued customer with the knowledge that I was lost in a Transylvanian forest, I pressed on. To my dismay, I was riding one of the horses in training that was just as clueless about the trails as I seemed to be. My plan to just loosen the reins and let the horse guide me home was no longer one of my options since my horse was not only incredibly tall (causing a pleasant effect between my face and the many low hanging branches and leaves) but he was also clumsy. Not that the rain mixing with the forest floor made it any easier for my horse to carry himself for more than a few feet without his hooves slipping in the thick mud.

The thickness of the branches and denseness of the bushes and leaves became too much for the two of us to manage on horseback so I decided the best decision was to dismount and lead the horses through the worst of it and then remount and ride the rest of the way home. Assuming I knew where "home" was, that is.

The rain became worse and worse and my horse's metal shoes were sliding in the muck at every hill and steep drop. I was comforted by the fact that the horse my female customer had been saddled with was a veteran of the trails and knew exactly where to put his feet and how to carry his weight as well as hers through the extremities of the conditions. To me, that was the most important factor. After all, I had never been worried about my safety while riding an unfamiliar horse. I had fallen off enough times and ended up in the hospital enough times to have learned how to keep my butt in the saddle and help the horse out when it needed help. And boy did my horse need help.

I decided the rain was too much for us to continue to walk so I waited for the girl to remount her horse before I attempted to hop on my own. I had mounted thousands of tall horses in my life and had always been thankful for my long legs, especially since out in the Transylvanian wilderness there wasn't a mounting block to be found. However, what I hadn't counted on was the difficulty of mounting on a tall and nervous horse while the pouring rain created a slippery effect on the leather saddle and slick boots and ski pants I had unthinkingly adorned that morning. After a great length of trying and failing to remount my horse, finally against all odds I managed to pull myself into place.

I had always been great at keeping situations comical and positive so when I decided to be honest to my one and only customer and tell her that I was lost—but not to worry because she would now have one hell of a story to tell her husband when we got back to the barn—all she could do was laugh. "Usually we charge extra for this," I turned in my stirrups so I could look the woman in the face as I spoke, "we call it the 'Adventure Trail Package.' But since I like you so much this one's on the house," I joked and she laughed some more.

I knew the trail that we had come on so instead of risking it any further in the heavy forest and persistence of the rain (since at this point both our light jackets and bare hands were not only soaked to the very core but our entire bodies were frozen to the bone) we decided to simply turn around and go back the way we had come.

Knowing if I dismounted my horse again I surely would not be able to get back on so I decided we would remain seated in the saddle and risk the ride through the low hanging branches and water covered leaves. I joked and laughed with the girl the entire ride home. When we arrived safely at the stables (well after my boss had returned with his customers on their trail and had already driven the streets in a panic looking for me) I finally dismounted from my horse. I gave him a big pat and an even bigger hug only to realize for the first time the many leaves that covered not only his mane and his back but the leaves had somehow managed to stick themselves into the crevices of my saddle as well. I also realized just how many leaves were on my own body. I looked to the face of my one and only customer, desperately hoping to see an expression on her face that would be anything other than annoyance, anger, or unhappiness with my efforts.

The woman who had been riding with me dismounted from her horse and began to laugh as she realized just how many leaves covered her horse and as well as herself. Her husband raced to her side, and I couldn't help but worry as he approached his wife, overly happy to see her returning after her brief time missing. The look on my boss's face as he watched didn't help my nervousness in the matter.

With a big smile stretched on the woman's face, she said to her husband, "Man do I have a story to tell you!"

****

Eager to put my Driver's License to good use, I was more than willing to slip into the driver's seat of my boss's beat-up Jeep. Although I was convinced the vehicle was older than myself, the circumstances proved that the time had come. I was going to drive the Jeep the few kilometers distance from the farm in order to retrieve the customers' "mineral water."

I started the engine of the Jeep with minor difficulties (not having understood fully what my boss had meant when he said it was a diesel engine and needed a minute to start). After cranking the key a few times the engine revved to life and I inhaled a deep breath as I gripped the steering wheel.

"Are you ready for this?" I said to no one in particular as my two feet maneuvered the clutch and gas pedal as I had been instructed.

Ok, ok. My long-ago life back in America had been filled with many a road trip and a clean driving record and never an accident to my truck's bumper or name, but the thought of driving a stick-shift for the first time in my life in a foreign country with my boss's vehicle was enough to make me on full alert.

After a few cautious minutes spent maneuvering the Jeep across bridges with no side rail and steep drops, loose pigs, and horses racing in the streets and gypsy children playing near the road, I finally reached my destination. I smiled, proud of my beforehand untested ability to shift from first to second gear and having accomplished the task so easily. Ok, not "so" easily...but I did it and for me, that was enough.

I step out of the dusty vehicle and retrieved the empty water jugs from the back seats. My feet crunched the gravel stones beneath me as I trekked my way down the hill toward the small river running through the small village of Prod. I reached the river and unscrewed the lid off the first bottle. I placed the empty container beneath a small rubber pipe that was protruding from the ground. An endless supply of "mineral water" streamed rhythmically from the tube as my bottle began to fill.

I took in a deep breath of the cool Romanian air as my eyes flickered at the small river inches from my feet. The villagers watched me with strange looks on their faces as they herded their livestock into the water in front of me. The dirty animals splashed and drank from the chilling water, eager for the taste.

Realizing the first of many of my water jugs had finished filling with the customer's "mineral water" I twisted the cap back on and reach for the next empty jug.

****

The snow crunched beneath my horse's hooves. I had been guiding trails for nearly three months now and winter had managed to creep up on me. It was December, close to Christmas and I was leading a group of city-goers, some local Romanian riders enjoying their Christmas holidays together on a weekend getaway. They were some of my "regulars" and in my short timespan working as a trail guide, they'd already visited four times. It seems word had spread like wildfire that an American Coach was running the yard and before I knew it I had attracted quite a few dressage and jumping enthusiasts to this yard in the middle of nowhere.

My horse's hooves clattered as we tread on the cobblestones. The snow hadn't fully stuck and was scattered here and there as we entered the small Transylvanian village. We had filled our bellies that morning with lots of garlic on toast—garlic is one of the main ingredients in many Transylvanian dishes. I wasn't sure if the legends of vampires being thwarted by garlic had led the people in Transylvania to eat so much of the stuff... or if it was the other way around. Maybe it was *because* the locals ate so much garlic that the vampire-hunters started carrying garlic?

A shiver ran down my spine, even though I was officially vampire-proof. The snowfall had made this small Romanian village eerily silent. My heart pounded as the sound of my horse's hooves sliced through the silence. I had ridden through this particular village dozens of times. It was extremely off-the-grid. So much so that it didn't even appear on Google Maps, something I hadn't imagined possible in this day and age.

I had the impression this particular village was trapped in a time bubble. The locals dressed in medieval style clothes. The men used carts pulled by horses, not cars, to transport the logs and firewood. The women wore bandanas on their heads to cover their hair, their long skirts were worn and ragged.

Although the villagers didn't run us outsiders out of town upon sight, we weren't exactly embraced with warm, welcome smiles. The piercing silence, garlic in my stomach, snow, and cobblestone streets only added to my nervousness. I was in charge of a group of about 10 advanced riders, and although we needed to keep a walk as we rode through the village, I didn't intend to stick around for long.

My horse walked beside one of the small farmhouses as I looked around, cautious not to stir anyone inside.

And then it happened.

A loud, piercing scream echoed from inside the walls of the barn beside us. I jumped in my saddle, panic taking over. Luckily for me, the group of riders didn't flinch at the sound of the blood-curdling squeal. They were Romanians after all.

"It's ok, Krystal," one of the men riding closely behind me called out. "It's just a pig!"

"A pig?!" I shrieked, my eyes refusing to leave the closed barn doors and source of the scream.

"Yes, it's nearly Christmas. That means it's the pig-killing season." The man shrugged as if surprised I didn't already know this.

In the distance, another scream could be heard. Again I jolted, though my horse remained steady. I took a deep breath, trying my hardest to keep myself together.

As we rode through the village, I realized that a pool of blood had already begun streaming from the various houses and into the streets.

"There's no such thing as vampires, there's no such thing as vampires, there's no such thing..." I mumbled to my horse. "I hope we're having garlic for dinner," I called to the group as I led them through the fray.

They laughed, though I wasn't sure if they got my joke.

****

Accidentally getting hired to work in Romania after being in the country for only two days was a welcome surprise for me. And I was forever thankful for my time there. I was amazed by Romania. As a child growing up in California, I could remember seeing fences around every piece of land. Even if there were no animals inside and it was nothing but open spaces and rolling hills and empty fields, for some reason it was always surrounded with harsh looking barb wire fences. I used to wonder as a kid what it would be like to live in a place with absolutely no fences. Just open space and freedom.

I found my childhood dream turn into a reality in Romania. We rode the horses absolutely anywhere and everywhere we pleased. Through villages, through forests, on the road... hell, I can even recall riding the horses to the pub once to allow my customers the chance to buy a round of drinks before heading back to the stables. What amazed me, even more, was the fact that there were no fences to be found.

Everywhere was unlimited space and openness. I was also surprised to discover that the villagers who owned livestock such as pigs or cows or horses didn't fence them in either. Sometimes the horses would be tied to a stake buried deep in the ground, allowing them to walk within the parameter to eat the grass. More often than not I saw the animals running wild and loose, only to wander back inside the village in the evening where their meal awaited them. Even the shepherds were herding the sheep by using dogs, something I had only seen in movies.

I had found myself in horse-heaven and I enjoyed every minute of it. I lived in Romania for 6 months in total, working at two different riding clubs. I trained horses, took customers out on long rides, competed in show jumping competitions, gave riding lessons, and yes, even got to partake in a real Hollywood film.

So the next time you're on vacation, and a friendly face offers you a job... why not take a chance, follow your heart and see where you end up? You might find yourself atop a Jackal, in a place without fences and memories that last a lifetime.

Desert to the Atlantic

BY AMANDA CHAMPERT

It is February and winter in the vast Moroccan desert, the days are hot and at night I can feel the cool air on my cheeks; everyone around me is wearing their winter hats during our dinners under our communal tent. Decorated in a patchwork of colors, greens, yellows, and reds, all sewn together by a thread that shone from our gas light. Our faces illuminated by the same light all perched over our bowls of soup, the warmth of the liquid warming me up from within.

We are all here under this tent because of a common goal to reach the Atlantic coast in a month. This is a journey that I will share with them and thirteen Barb-Arab stallions through one of the harshest landscapes on earth. The desert had a way of putting everything back into perspective, the immensity of it all, the horizon stretching out in all directions for miles. This adventure would lead me to achieve one of my longest rides so far, 543 miles (875kms).

Adventure Awaits

It was mid-December when I received a phone call, just a normal day carrying my shopping home.

France is home for me, surrounded by the crystal blue waters of the Côte d'Azur, a very different landscape to the one I would experience very soon. I knew I had to answer, the number that was calling only meant one thing; Adventure awaits. I put down my bag and pressed the answer button; a very short but effective phone conversation...

The voice on the phone said, "Hello Amanda, How are you?"

"I'm great thank you and you?!"

"What would you say to a month on horseback in the Moroccan desert? I know you will say yes, so pack your bags and camera."

The voice was right, I had already accepted his challenge when I had seen his number pop up on my phone. This ride had never been achieved by anyone in Morocco, this sent chills down my spine, it would be a journey that would push my limits and inspire others to take the same path next year. To travel across the Saharan desert on horseback especially, as this trail would lead me to witness with my own eyes the borders between Morocco and Algeria, heavily guarded by military forces on both sides added another layer of thrill to the whole journey.

As tradition has it, all trips like these has a WhatsApp group, exchanging all our riding stories before meeting in person. These exchanges scared me more than the upcoming ride; all life long riders and great adventurers themselves; riding along the Mongolian plains, 1000km across Europe, and vast knowledge of every breed of horse. I was in awe by these cavaliers, I could not wait to meet them but it just augmented this feeling that I was maybe a little bit out of my depth… but I quickly comforted myself by the knowledge that I knew the horses that I would be riding. The very same ones that I had learned on, spending hours in the ring with my master horseman that gave me his total patience and then some until all the basics and more had been mastered. Getting off my horse after every lesson felt like I had lost the ability to walk, my legs had forgotten how to hold my weight but I knew that even if I awoke sore the next day, I would find the strength to get back in the saddle and carry on.

I then think to myself, I am crazy to have accepted but I was putting doubt in myself; I had come so far in so very little time, I was ready and quickly found that even with years of experience, a trip like this can put fear into anyone. The thirst for new places, to learn, and to share all that with a horse makes it all worthwhile. I soon forget any fear that I may have had in the first few hours of riding. It was not about the destination, it was about those moments in between, an accumulation of those to make a whole.

Preparation

It is actually happening!
Still at home and looking down at my suitcase contemplating if I was really doing this. What do you pack for a whole month? I was very conscious that I couldn't just wash my clothes or bring an endless supply of riding jodhpurs.

I concluded that it didn't matter, I would turn things inside out if needed and, well, I had already experienced first hand that it honestly didn't matter if things started to smell a little. Our clothes start to take on a gritty texture and turn a color of sand after a few days, as if we'd all started rolling around on the ground!

Arriving in Ouarzazate. The last major town before entering the desert, a very strange looking place; long alleys with terracotta buildings lining them. For such a large area with hundreds of neighborhoods, there were very few people around, it seemed derelict. A town of passage; many here are heading somewhere else, stocking up on everything they may need for their trip, for me it was the last place I'd see civilization until the following month.

The moment where I met all the faces I'd be sharing this month with, I distinctively remember that everyone looked very clean, freshly shaven, hair washed, the scent of perfume on their best clothes, we enjoyed our first couscous together at the hotel before returning to our rooms. I spent an excessive amount of time in the bath that night... I knew that it would be something that I would crave when my skin, irritated by the sand and dust, would long to feel the touch of the warm water of a shower to wash it all off.

The next morning, I got dressed all ready to ride that afternoon. Riding pants, chaps, comfy and brand new riding shoes, helmet, and my little blue riding polo. Ready, set, go!

On the Road

Five hours to go until I would set eyes upon the horses. A great time to spend to get to know everyone on the minibus, still all looking pristine in their riding gear. It became apparent straight away that we were all a little quirky and an eccentric group.

A couple reminded me of two cowboys from the far west, mostly because of their hats with feathers on the side beaten and worn out from their many rides in Mongolia. They traveled from New Zealand and were very much looking forward to riding Barb-Arabs for the first time.

A couple with all the gadgets, a very tall broad man with an excessive amount of knowledge tucked under his riding helmet, and a cute small, short-haired lady who even with many years of riding experience had been convinced by her husband that this was a trip of a lifetime. Still not quite sure if she'd made the right decision to participate but excited nonetheless.

A lady from the land of the Lord of the Rings; New Zealand she had me hooked the moment she started chatting, and I didn't stop hearing her fun bubbly voice the entire month. The one with all the jokes... every group needs a person like this!

A British—but now converted to American, as she put it—lady with humor and quirkiness, and with the best looking riding boots, also joined our team. I didn't know it yet, but she would save me halfway through the trip.

A Canadian lady, what is the saying... no one can dislike a Canadian? Totally true! A photographer and writer, a true adventuress herself. I can thank her for the beautiful photos that she took of me. For once I appeared in photos instead of just behind the lens.

A sweet and kind gentleman from Sweden... I shall call him the medicine man.

A gentle German lady, who for the entire trip always seemed to have the perfect hair, usually tied up in a plat and always last in the group whilst riding due to her slow horse, Bahar.

Finally, our guide, a slim Moroccan man with such a friendly smile and who was quite cheeky, looking to either tease someone or make them burst out loud with laughter.

Our band of cavaliers was complete and still very unsure of what we would all face during this trip but one thing was sure, I would experience something magical with them all in the weeks to come.

So it Begins

This is it! The horses are in view from my seat on the minibus. The landscape already desert, in every direction sand, the only element out of sorts is the thirteen Barb-Arab stallions, their coats a stark contrast from the coral color all around them.

Our guide sits us all down for our first mint tea, a very important moment in the day. The tea. He takes a sip and then asks us all individually with a cheeky smile about our riding experiences, noting down our names and placing little minus or plus signs next to them. It felt like a test, going back to school; what should I say I wondered to get the prize... This he explains is to select a horse for each of us according to our pre-diagnosed level, to be tested during the next few hours.

My turn to speak.

"Well I'm no expert but what I know is what you've taught me. So it is up to you to judge but I think I have improved considerably since you last saw me on a horse." The guide is the master horseman that I spoke of before. He just smiled at me and said "Moonlight is for you then." A proud little moment for me as it was an "upgrade" and a challenge in one. I couldn't wait to mount on!

Setting off from just outside of Merzouga, in the region of Erg Chebbi; a huge expanse of dunes, that just stretches out for miles, disappearing into the horizon like a mirage. The color of the sand, almost orange, shining from the sun, beating down from above. The sight captivated me, the size of it... instantly feeling incredibly small and insignificant from the magnitude of what time and nature had created over the centuries but also eroded. The sand encroaching itself throughout the landscape, gaining space each year. It certainly made me question where all this sand came from? Where it would end up and what it may look like in future centuries to come.

For today our horses had all been tacked up ready to set off straight away. I head over to Moonlight who had his eyes closed bathing in the rays of the afternoon sun. I stroke his muzzle to wake him a little also saying hello at the same time. Popping my water bottle in the saddlebag, I untie him from a very prickly bush, which didn't seem to bother him as he starts nibbling on it, however, this made my task of setting him free a little tricky, trying to avoid impaling myself. Bringing him away from the bush, I mount up and adjust my stirrups as whoever had ridden him before had extremely long legs.

I'm all set and I can feel that Moonlight is also rearing to go, feeling his muscles tense up beneath me. I'd say he was the smallest of the group, with the kindest look in his eyes but with a little sparkle of cheekiness; remembering a detail that he was a stallion like all the horses in this group with the exception of three. This means they would be competing with each other for dominance... this was most apparent when we set off. A couple of the horses tried to nip the horse in front, one even reared up on his hind legs almost setting off the entire group into a canter. Holding onto my reins this was not the moment to set off at high speeds... everyone was still getting to know their steeds and mounting stallions for the first time. Even great riders have "first times" still. My little Moonlight during all this behaved; mostly. He was just excited to move.

The time is 16:45, quite late and still being winter, the days are short. The sun was already setting, its position in the sky hitting me square in the eyes, almost blinding me, the strength of the light piercing through every fiber of my body. Squinting, I try to see the path in front but it was impossible. I had to trust Moonlight to follow but it seemed even he was having a hard time, diverging from left to right, his head bent towards the ground; trying to avoid the beam of light. Despite the difficulty of vision, seeing everything in the form of a silhouette is incredible, especially in a landscape like this one.

The only shapes I can see, are the horses; the ground below is flat, the dust on the ground being kicked up by forty-eight hooves; creating a dance between the earth and us.

An hour into the ride, our first canter. On a small track, a mix of sand and small rocks. One behind the other. Moonlight full of energy trying to over-take the horse in front, Atlas. He was trying to be cheeky but I needed to let him know who was in charge, he was testing me and I was testing him. Loosening the reins and tightening them again just at the right moments, his little bubbly and intelligent character shining through. We both knew we had to find a status quo, that moment we both clicked, finding our rhythm it felt like we were flying through the desert. It was such a smooth ride. I felt like I was riding on air. That was the moment I fell in love with him, we'd synchronized and I wasn't going to let him down for the next twenty-nine days and he wasn't going to either.

Our First Desert Stars

The sun was falling below the horizon, suddenly the warm air that had warmed my skin had disappeared replaced by a breeze that brushed over my skin. Little goosebumps dotted my arms.

I pulled out my jumper from the saddlebag, the wool still warm from the heat of the day. Once the sun had gone it felt like I'd changed to another country, I'd soon need more layers if the temperature continued to drop.

Soon, I couldn't see further than Moonlight's ears bobbing up and down in front of me. The first star appearing above, I had never ridden at night and none of the horses either, who were all getting a little agitated. Quickly reducing the space between the horse in front, sticking together like a band of lost boys in the desert... all neighing, communicating between themselves like us humans looking all around if we could spot the camp. Still nothing, it was truly dark.

The terrain had changed from flat ground, from what I could fathom from my saddle, using all my other senses, except my sight. A dried-up river bed, forming bumps on the ground, their shape outlined by the light created from the stars, there was no moon that night. It was peaceful, no one was speaking, hypnotized with their necks tilted up at the millions upon millions of stars above. It was impossible to count them; the sky was so bright compared to the landscape below. At this moment I could have probably heard a pin drop, sound seemed to travel differently here. Even the sound of the hooves seemed quiet. The vastness of the desert created a sort of vacuum where even a whisper seemed loud. It certainly made me wish I knew more about the cosmos, trying to reach deep into my memories if I could remember the constellations, only one came to mind it was the Ursa Major; the giant bear, to spot it I looked all around, it was in the East emerging from the ground, I could have observed it for hours. I was pulled out of my dream-like state by a less natural light beaming straight in front almost blinding me, my eyes had adapted to the darkness... it was the 4x4 indicating camp was just there! The time was 9pm and the distance seventeen kilometers, we'd arrived at camp one.

Feet hitting the soft ground, I wobbled a little unsure of what to do next and my legs were slow to react to the fact that I needed them again. Untying the girth of my saddle, I place it on the mat in camp removing the reins and leaving the halter. Looking all around in the dark, I try to spot a place to park Moonlight but I quickly realize there are no trees in sight, not that I could see much...

A voice somewhere lost in the darkness shouts "Look on the ground, there are spikes with a loop to pass the rope." Scanning the ground, bingo! Making a quick-release knot, I run off in the direction of the feed, stubbing my toe on one of those hidden spikes, I felt my toe throbbing but I had to get water and food to bring back to Moonlight; I take a deep breath and I carry on.

Nose diving into the bucket, Moonlight was obviously quite hungry, putting his entire weight on his rope, and almost taking me with him. My stomach was also making musical notes, I would probably do the same, smelling the soup coming from the kitchen just made my mouth water. I check one last time that everything was ok with Moonlight and give him a goodnight cuddle and I head off in the direction where I believe I'd find my bag and a tent still in the pouch.

I pick a spot and lay out my tent. Challenge number one of this long journey was putting up a tent in the dark with only a small head torch. Looking around me, everyone else was bent over their tents, little moving lights frantically trying to find how the tents functioned. Hearing a few exclamations of frustration... I hammered the last spike into the ground with a very large rock. There it was: my home for the night. Throwing my bag in and then myself after, I lay on the floor of my tent, letting out a large breath, taking a moment to organize my thoughts about the events of the day. This truly was going to be like no other ride I'd been on...

I wander out of my tent and located the cooks' kitchen, which wasn't too difficult to find, the smell coming from it only made my stomach rumble even more. Letting the smell lead me, I could hear the rustling of hay that the horses were eating as I passed. Tucking my nose into the kitchen my senses are hit by the extraordinary mix of Moroccan spices. Delicious!

The cook smiles up at me and says in French, "Tu as faim?" Are you hungry? I just wanted to nose dive into the plate like Moonlight.

The cook was singing along to a tune while he plated up the food, to be carried to the communal tent where the others were waiting. My first meal under the stars was a soup to die for, a vegetable Tajine which I think everyone agreed there wasn't enough of. I made a personal note in my head to ask him to make another. I'd never seen such a colorful plate, the taste of the vegetables mixed with a combination of those magic spices. I ate so much, I thought my stomach would burst!

Belly's full, one by one we all said goodnight. Laying in my tent, I slowly closed my eyes with a smile on my face. I couldn't wait to wake up the next morning to see the view from the door of my tent.

Fast Forward

Its been a week since I started my journey into the desert. During this time, I had changed my horse, I was no longer riding Moonlight but now Atlas. There had been an exchange between myself and the cheerful Kiwi Lady, she needed to ride a calmer horse. She had been atop Najm, a fiery Barb-Arab with a lot of spirit that proved to be little too stubborn. I had exchanged with the second guide. I was now astride a gentle giant who loved snuggles when I came to tack him up in the mornings.

Today is Saturday, tomorrow we arrive in Zagora in the Drâa Valley. The first town to indicate on its borders Tombouctou 52 days. Famous as a trading route from Morocco to Mali during the 14th Century to trade in salt, gold, ivory, and slaves. However, that's not the direction I'm going in… So far, we had been carried one hundred and fifty miles in six days.

What a truly incredible week, the group; myself included had fallen into a routine, departing each morning at seven-thirty. Efficiency was my second name by the time Saturday came. Waking up, dressed, tent down, eating breakfast, and tacking up Atlas. Breakfast was my favorite moment, our Kiwi cowboy was the only one with a signal on his phone and had become a sort of anchorman announcing the news, or conducting research for a question from someone else in the group. In his accent, he would say, "In today's news hour, we have..." A perfect way to put a smile on my face.

After breakfast I would sneak into the kitchen. I'd grab a little snack to put in my saddle bag for me and Atlas, usually some bread from last night's dinner and fruit for me.

Most days lunch was far away. We were both clocking up on average twenty-five miles each day. Sore had taken on a whole new meaning. In the morning, reaching up and sitting back in the saddle, I'd wonder if my butt had disappeared. I couldn't feel it anymore until suddenly a sensation would come back. I would start shifting in my saddle uncomfortably until I had to change position completely adopting the position that would help a little while. If that didn't work, I would walk alongside Atlas until my feet had had enough of the rocks massaging them vigorously.

I had days where energy was low, it was like Atlas knew and would cheer me right up, bumping his muzzle into my shoulder as if to say come on. I could also feel when he was lacking in fuel, giving him his snack, letting him stretch by walking beside him, he loved it when I would stroke his little chin groove and crest. If I stopped he'd ask for me to continue. In these moments any fatigue was forgotten. He was the best traveling partner.

The landscapes so far had never been the same from one day to the next, the only thing consistent was a lot of sand and rocks! Imagine large expanses of land as far as you can see in the morning it was a Reg (rocky desert) with the horizon filled with mountains usually the direction of lunch or camp. The land was barren, dotted by a few Acacia trees or shrubs so dry that I was sure were quite dead.

A few dromedaries walking off into the distance upon seeing us coming would often change their direction. The most surprising is the people we'd come across, walking or on a donkey heading who knows where. I'd try and guess... weekly shop, tea with their neighbors, or migrating north as it was a large region of Nomads moving as the weather would get hotter. Life was simple but tough out here, every person we'd pass would enquire about our caravan of horses and why we were traveling across the desert with no apparent purpose. This would often confuse them, it wasn't natural to just wander around in the desert for pleasure.

A way we had decided to pass time was trying to spot the kitchen tent, a way of knowing if the camp was nearby for lunch! The white fabric was the only thing out of sorts in the decor, testing who had the best vision, even the horses could spot camp, speeding up their pace as a group. They often knew before us all, their intelligence was mind-blowing.

This morning as usual my alarm was hearing the giggling from the tent next to mine; six-thirty AM and the girls, the Canadian and American with those amazing boots would always crack up with laughter the moment their eyes would open. Everyone could hear them, which meant we all started laughing from our tents individually not knowing what we were laughing about. However, this particular morning I knew that from our camp there was still 40 miles to reach Zagora, almost impossible. The weather had gradually been getting hotter as the days went by, every day leaving camp earlier and earlier to avoid the hottest part of the day. Today was a day that would leave a mark on myself and the entire group. Our guide even let out a sigh of relief when seeing the tents!

Setting off, I see a road being constructed. The first sign of civilization, though it was unclear why a road was being laid in the middle of nowhere with no obvious destination. Even in the most remote places in Morocco, the country was rapidly changing. Roads meant progress for our guides. As Europeans, our conversation was drawn more into the topic of preserving nature, quite conscious of our impact on the Earth.

Men were working in their trucks, what I love most about Moroccan culture is their friendliness, always saying hello, a customary "La bes?" (How are you?) The way they talk amongst strangers is as if you'd been life long friends. Moroccans love to talk about everything and nothing!

"SNAKE!" Someone shouts out from the front. Snakes here were not the kind that I wanted to come nose to nose with.

"What is it?" Everyone in the group started asking; a Horned Viper, venomous, yet not lethal, but still very painful.

I did not want to accidentally step on one, as they are camouflaged brilliantly in their habitat. Yet, I was curious to see what it looked like, having only seen them in zoos, it is always wonderful witnessing a species in their own home. Unfortunately, by the time I had reached the spot, it had slithered away most probably under a rock and there were many of those at my feet for it to hide under. The horses were unfazed, probably used to seeing a lot of creatures slithering away, and carried on with their forward march.

Lunch that day was over very quickly, arriving at mid-day and setting off again at 1pm. I sat under the only tree, an Acacia. The feeling of shade today would be rare, so I lapped up the last cool feeling on my face before we had to head off again.

We carry on along a flat mountain pass to join the Drâa Valley on the other side, the land was empty of people and without vegetation, just rocks of all sizes. No sound except for the very hot wind whistling, carrying the dust straight into my face, I could feel the grit sticking to my skin. It was like going to the spa every day, I was starting to resemble a blonde scarecrow. Reaching the summit, we had a magnificent view of below, Atlas wasn't to keen on approaching the edge, it was very high up. From up here, it felt like I was on top of the world, I could see we'd reached an area of agriculture, growing strangely in a place with no water, watermelons. The nets shining, the fruit growing under them so large it appeared to be lakes at first sight.

The ground around me was radiating heat even at this altitude, Atlas was sweating, his coat still a little thick for winter, he reminded me of one of those kind grandpas with a small beard just under his mouth, more Barb than Arab. He was looking at the rocks below our feet, here they were all black, it felt like being on another planet, such a sight that I half expected an astronaut to come walking along in front of us. Heading down the valley we borrow a small trail niched into the rock face perfectly maintained by the local population who use this path regularly; to navigate between the valleys, which seemed impenetrable to the untrained eye.

At this moment I discover how sure-footed our group of stallions are; the space between the rock face and the valley below so small that sitting in the saddle, I'd scarce wanted to look down. Looking straight ahead, I could see the track full of small rocks, big rocks, and dust that would move whenever the hooves of Atlas would walk over them. At certain points, he would need to climb down large steps and would drop dramatically, leaning way back in my saddle to avoid falling forward. There was just enough space to get off at one intersection, I decided to walk in front, leading Atlas by the reins to the valley floor. I realize I'd been holding my breath and I let it all out, relief rushing through me. Looking up at the mountain we'd just climbed down, the path no longer visible from below, utterly camouflaged in the rock and also very vertical. We could have easily missed the path and if we did, I imagine the only solution to get down or up would be to rock-climb or learn how to fly!

The day hadn't even reached the halfway mark, today was to be the longest but as of yet, I didn't know how long. I just kept one hoof in front of the other, admiring everything around me, even the rocks on the ground were beautiful. The floor shone with them, all different colors and in certain areas, I could spot little cylinder shells and fossils. This area was once the bottom of a sea, now gone, dried up by the encroaching desert... proof that this region was once rich in wildlife.

Humans had also left their mark through prehistoric markings engraved within certain rocks. Elephants, giraffes, fish even a Mammoth! Depicted alone or being hunted by skinny stick figure men with spears; what a sight it must have been, though it was hard to imagine now with all this heat and dust flying about. The only animals crossing our paths were herds of Dromedary, (camels) sheep or donkeys ridden by the very few locals doing a similar journey than us but not with the same intentions.

At this point we had been going at a steady pace all day, reaching the valley floor the ground opened up to a space so flat it was hard to believe I'd just been high up on a mountain ridge. A voice up front shouted in their Kiwi accent, "Get ready guys, cantering time!"

Instinctively, Atlas had already tensed up his muscles, I could feel it. Ears perked up, mentally he was cantering in his thoughts. I had hardly any time to think before we were zooming past everyone, swerving between the shrubbery, overtaking the others going faster and faster. I was free and so was Atlas after enduring thousands of rocks he was apparently as relieved and excited as I was to be cantering off into the horizon. That feeling of flying through the air, it was like having air-conditioning; it felt incredible after the heat of the day.

I kept going, balancing in my saddle to feel as much adrenaline as possible and speed, now jumping over the bushes on the ground, almost letting Atlas take me where he wanted into the terrain. I wanted him to feel alive and free like I felt in this moment.

The light played with the dust being churred by the horses' hoofs, the scene straight out of a western movie, the only difference was that I was wearing a shesh (a desert scarf) to protect me from the sand rather than a cowboy hat. It was such a surreal moment, I had to pinch myself mentally, it was like I was having an out-of-body experience, not quite believing that I was there living through this epic journey. It could also have been the Moroccan sun that had been beating down on me all day, whatever it was, I realized that this trip was having a profound effect on me. The desert was turning me into a true equestrian adventuress.

The moment the canter stopped I just wanted to head off again, Atlas still itching to carry on, I had to make him turn on a circle to make him slow down and to calm his spirits.

I took a look down at my GPS, I did a double-take. It had been eight hours since we'd left camp that morning. Veins pumping with adrenaline, any moment now I would come down from my high and be hit by a massive wave of fatigue and nausea. The heat was not agreeing with me, my body was craving cool air, I started to feel disconnected from everything, I needed to get off but stayed on for as long as I could. I could see some larger shrubs ahead big enough to create some shade; I told myself if I reach them everything will be better... I am a few meters away now but I can go no further. I shout out that I needed to stop. Before I fall off, I jump off Atlas, it wasn't my most graceful dismount, almost face-planting the ground.

I wander over to some shade taking Atlas with me. I collapse under a small tree and place my head between my knees, trying to breathe, wishing the dizziness away. I was experiencing my first heatstroke, I felt cold yet hot at the same time. I could feel Atlas putting his muzzle in my hair like he knew something was wrong, trying to comfort me the only way he knew how. In the distance, I hear footsteps approaching and I see my favorite riding boots appear. A hand reaches out with two magical pills, to fix any ailment, I waited to feel the effects. They worked quickly, I started to feel like myself again, emerging from my state I look up and see the American; my savior smiling up at her, she had changed my fate of being unable to finish the ride for today. It would have been devastating to call the assistance vehicle to take me to camp.

Standing back up, I swing back into my saddle finding the strength to carry on, Atlas using his intelligence to follow the others without me giving him any indications on what to do, that moment I was more passenger than a rider. He kept on impressing me, it was like having moral support saying come on, not much further!

Looking ahead, my eyes taking a moment to adjust, I could see an emerald green palm grove. It covered such a large area that I couldn't tell where it ended, all this growth in the middle of the desert. A haven of life, there would be water, people, and wildlife ahead. A stark contrast of what we had seen all day. Colorful birds chirping, singing their unique tunes nestled on the palm leaves, running water irrigating the fields hidden under the olive and date trees. Children finishing school in awe of the thirteen horses suddenly appearing in sight following us on their bikes or running along beside us. They asked our names, those of our horses, and a million other questions. We carry on reaching an area where a group of teenagers were playing a football game, (soccer) the dust being kicked all over. Illuminated by the dusk a simple scene made extraordinary by the light setting over them.

We had all been stunned into silence after an entire week of only seeing our band of riding companions suddenly, being plunged back into reality. The most simple human activities had us all fascinated. We couldn't be far now from our camp, yet we still ride deeper into the palm grove, the last rays of the sun were disappearing as we were again riding in the dark. I was following the noises of the horse in front of me, all I could see was the little white ears of Atlas. I had been lost in thought when suddenly I realized that all the horses in front of me had stopped. I hadn't heard Abdel, our guide, say we'd arrived, even Atlas nearly bumped into the bum of another horse. Quickly realizing his placement was not the best, he backed up a little.

As I was still a little light-headed from earlier, I take a moment to connect my thoughts to my body to slide down my saddle, my movements all in slow motion. My feet touched the ground and using Atlas to hold me up, I take a moment to make my first step and then another. Leading Atlas and following the others, I was functioning on auto-pilot.

Arriving in camp, I see that my little tent had been already been put up, I take Atlas to a palm tree and give him his feed, everyone in the group working in silence. I take my bag and crash into my tent, closing my eyes falling asleep but I was pulled out from my slumber by the scent of food, Suddenly realizing I was hungry, my belly making all sorts of rumbling acoustic sounds, I scramble out of my tent and trusted my nose to lead me in the right direction.

I found everyone collapsed into our little camping chairs, all with vacant expressions on their faces. No one had found the courage to wash it seemed, hair sticking up in all directions, and chaps still zipped up.

Finally, Mr. Gadget uttered the words, "How many miles did we do?"

Looking down at my GPS my eyes opening wide not believing the numbers displayed; we'd traveled thirty-five miles in eleven and a half hours. No wonder everyone still looked as if they were sitting in their saddles. Everyone was numb and still lost in the desert. Pulled back from our thoughts, in came the largest Tajine of Keftas (meat balls) served with couscous, the first bite and everyone started to come back to life. Conversations started up and laughter filled the tent. One at a time we started to retreat to our tents, bellies full. I place my head on my pillow and fall into the deepest sleep.

Sand Everywhere

The next morning, I find Brahim re-shoeing Atlas. Walking on the rocks had taken its toll on all the shoes of the horses. I watched him from beginning to end, it was like watching a pedicure, the only thing missing was a color polish. Atlas throughout was nibbling away on his breakfast, almost unaware of what was happening, cool as a cucumber as usual. The camp was surrounded by Argan trees, still not ready for picking. As we approached the Atlantic, the landscape had been changing from arid to green pastures; passing through villages and empty roads always long and melting into the scenery. We had traveled more than half our journey and still had seventy-seven miles to go and three days to do it in. Each lunch break is like heaven being able to hide under a tree.

One lunch I had tied Atlas a little close to the table that we ate and he quickly popped his head over the shoulder of the Kiwi cowboy to take a bite from his plate with an expression of complete innocence on his face. After everyone had a good chuckle I wandered over and extracted him from the plate and shortened the rope a little. He continued to observe the scene from his lunch laid out on the ground.

Lunch had become the holy grail for me. One fateful day we had diverged slightly in the wrong direction. We were not lost but our guide had extended our morning ride by a few hours thinking that passing through the mountain would be the shorter option. Trailing through what must have been where water would run down the mountain to reach the summit. My head emerged from behind the last boulder, I had a 180° view of the valley below. We had found where we needed to get to, even spotting the 4x4. The crew were probably wondering what we were doing all the way up there but they were also relieved to see our little group considering we were extremely late for lunch! Like the white rabbit from Alice in Wonderland, I had become very attached to being on time, for food...

It was already about 4pm and our stomachs were more empty than the dried-up river beds surrounding us. The water was also running low... one problem there was no obvious path to get down, Abdel had already searched the mountain. Finally, finding what could be used as a path, our guide contemplating for at least an hour the best way to navigate the treacherous path. Deciding to explore on foot to see if it was safe and also removing rocks that could be dangerous, he ran back up at lightning speed. All clear.

Everyone had to get off their horse, it was so steep that even the horses usually unfazed by heights suddenly had a case of vertigo! Myself included. I made it a point to reassure Atlas at the same time, which actually helped me with my own sudden fear of heights! I made the small mistake of looking down, nope I mustn't do that, it was a long way down. I couldn't see where the slope ended…

I decided to focus on where I put my feet and kept repeating "Yalla," meaning "GO" in Arabic to Atlas who seemed to respond well to me showing him that I wasn't scared. A horse has a sense for picking up fear from their rider and I certainly didn't want him panicking on this ridge! My legs trembled as the ground felt very unstable under my feet. I needed to stop to take a breath, watching the others head down with their horses one by one. Everyone made it down and we all look at each other in victory. Everyone started clapping, smiling, and cheering… what a great sensation. It was pure adrenaline coursing through our bodies, including our horses with sweat dripping from under their saddles.

Using that adrenaline, we walk on to the 4x4 who was there waiting with water and food. The time was 5pm. Lunch was ready and we all collapsed like sacks of potatoes around our plates of food. It was the quietest lunch we'd eaten. I was personally still up on that ridge thinking about how amazing yet quite daunting that moment was, not knowing if we could get down and possibly having to turn back. Yet I was here munching away on my pasta, now safe in the valley that I had seen from above.

I took a moment to lay down, probably resembling some sort of half-dead starfish. The kind medicine man pulled me out of my current state, we still had to make camp. I trudged back over to Atlas with a very large piece of bread and a bucket of water to give him some energy. We both head back out into the landscape, now walking along the foot of the mountain. Luckily as we had already covered the majority of the distance for the day, our camp wasn't far. That day our tents had already been put up, what an amazing team! I think at that moment I just wanted to cry with joy on seeing my little red tent. Letting Atlas loose from the reins, brushing him, and giving his very much deserved food, I let him rest. All the whilst grooming him, I found myself talking to him, babbling away about the day, his ears perked up listening. We made quite a team, him and I. Both of us sturdy and more resilient than first imagined.

That night we were visited by four children seemingly appearing from nowhere. They had probably spotted us trotting up to camp. They installed themselves just a few feet away, laying out a colorful cloth on the ground and placing over it, mini dromedary toys, jewelry made from hundreds of colors; they had come to sell their homemade crafts. Being the only one of the group with a notion of Arabic; I was commandeered to communicate with this little group. I approached them, a beautiful girl seemed to be the one in charge.

Saying hello, asking how she was, and her name, I spoke to her. She smiled at me, and then answered me in perfect French. She was one of the lucky ones with the opportunity to go to school. She started asking lots of questions about how we had ended up here and where we were going. Finally, we started to discuss if she'd made the cute dromedary she was selling. It was indeed her handy work and that of her mother. Full of sequins, made of different colored material, she tells me that everything is at twenty-five dirhams; about two euros fifty. At that price she sold them all!

It was time for a bucket shower, it had been approximately four days since my last one; I had always been too tired to wash the last few evenings. I carried my bucket of warm water to the shower tent, the feel of the water on my skin felt amazing, I came back to life. The smell of the soap made me dream about having that very first bath at the end of our trip. I was starting to crave the simplest mundane things, chocolate included in this. My craving had made it around the group as that night Abdel arrived in the tent with a tablet of chocolate. I savored that square letting it melt slowly on my tongue... I will never forget the taste of it, with a little sip of mint tea, I was in heaven.

Journeys End but Never Forgotten

The days are passing by at lightning speed now, approaching the final day. Every-night looking down at the map seeing how far I'd come, the line on the map stretching across from one side of the country the other.

Again a new landscape to explore, no more Argan trees, but beach like scapes. There are no more trees, most probably due to frequent winds coming from the Atlantic Ocean, the plants here were all hugging the ground. The strangest element hidden within these plants were hundreds of snails no longer inhabited, just their shells bleached by the sun. They must emerge on the rare occasions of rain and quickly dry out from the heat.

The weather here was truly bizarre, a sort of fog was forming coming off from the ground; mysterious. The light ethereal, a haze would stop me from seeing the landscape. The wind was getting stronger, grit between my teeth, we head off in the direction of our last camp. Passing through villages painted all white, the sky was grey; painting a rather sad landscape but at least it was cool. In this village, the women were all dressed in multi-colored skirts, signifying that they were Berber, the colors represented their status in their community. Beautiful head scarfs, some even wore black veils decorated with little pompoms and stitched with lots of different patterns representing crops, flowers, and the landscape of their home. As I passed by, they all smiled up at me and I would smile back, waving them goodbye.

The wind increasingly grew stronger as the day went by, making it hard to keep my eyes open. The sand flew into my eyes, my sunglasses no longer sufficient protection. A sand storm was approaching our location, we needed to pick up our speed to arrive at camp before it did. The horses, also not particularly enjoying the weather, started making all sorts of noises and trotting automatically as if annoyed by the weather.

We reach the camp before it was completely impossible to put our tents up; the sand was flying everywhere, a frantic struggle to get everything hooked in place before the wind picked up more speed, hammering the spikes into the ground.

Dinner that night had a very sandy taste and was truly crunchy; even the tea. That night everyone retreated to their tents rather early.

I was woken by the flapping of my tent, I had to get out and put everything back in place to avoid flying away. By getting out I let in a very large amount of sand which formed a rather thick layer once settled on my sleeping bag. Once outside, the sand on my skin stung whilst I tried to find the spike that had come loose. Trying to fix it as quickly as possible, I dive back into my tent and hide inside my sleeping bag.

I stayed wide awake listening to the wind, I have to admit I was a little scared; alone I started to talk to myself for reassurance that it would be ok until eventually, I fell asleep. When I awoke to the sound of the storm still raging outside I found myself sandwiched between the roof of my tent and the floor. I could hear shouting outside, I couldn't tell who it was but I had overslept not hearing my alarm over the wind. I emerged into a scene that resembled very much like I had been transported into the world of Mad Max whilst I slept.

Everything was flying everywhere, folding up my tent and getting ready in this was quite funny and yet rather frustrating as nothing would sit still long enough to be able to manage anything productive! Looking at the horses, all munching away they all seemed not to notice the weather. Breakfast was a little grittier than usual and my toothpaste was somewhat more corrosive. It was as if we were being kicked out. That ride to the beach was something to behold, the sand made it impossible to see anything around us. My camera at this point was well tucked away, I only have my memories of our last ride. The sand getting in every nook, making my eyes water; I thought to myself that months later I would probably still find sand from today. Suddenly, we stop; we had arrived at the beach though it was impossible to tell, I could not see two centimeters in front of me let alone the ocean that was right in front of me.

It was no longer important that I couldn't see the ocean... like I had thought at the beginning of this voyage. It was about all the moments in between and not the destination. I had experienced my first sand storm and it was fabulous; I'd even say it was a great way to finish this expedition.

I got down from Atlas, the feel of the soft sand beneath my riding boots, on the beach, 545 miles!

I am most definitely not the same person I was when I started this trip and neither was Atlas. Sharing this with him was eye-opening; the courage and trust a horse will put in a person. I had never built such a connection with a horse before, I was saddened by the fact it was over but also filled with so many emotions I scarce knew which one to process first. Was Atlas sad to see me go? I wondered. I didn't know the answer, but I am fascinated and impatient to see his reaction when we see each other again.

I think that this experience profoundly changed my perspective on life, what is important, and maybe an understanding of why we are here as human beings... to live. We can live in a world full of mysteries waiting to be sought out if willing to take a leap of faith. To push my limits and realizing after such an epic journey that it had opened up a whole new world for me and even if it was the end of this crusade to the ocean, it was potentially the beginning of a new one.

Adventures in Sicily

BY KRYSTAL KELLY

"What do you mean I CAN'T GET ON THE PLANE?!" I asked, trying not to raise my voice at the airline teller in front of me. I couldn't help it. I was on the brink of having a downright panic attack in the middle of the ticket counter at the airport.

"Your passport is blocked from being able to enter the country of Romania," the woman stated flatly. Her voice had no trace or hint of sympathy or empathy for my current situation.

"I'm aware of that. I still am not allowed to enter that country for another two months...but why can't I get on this plane? It's only going to France. Look at my itinerary," I stuffed my crinkled papers into her hands desperately. "See? I already booked a flight to take me from France to Italy. I'm not going anywhere near Romania!"

The lady scanned the papers uninterested. Without putting much effort into her decision she threw the papers back in my hands before adjusting her reading glasses on her face. With a bored look and a firm voice, she said to me, "That doesn't matter. You are not allowed to board this flight. If you want you can go home and rebook another flight, or you can cancel your flight to Romania via France and rebook another seat."

"Ok, then I'll cancel the small flight to Romania and keep my flight to Italy and France instead," I tried to come to a form of agreement. Anything but not boarding my flight to Italy, where I was supposed to start work the next day.

"You can't do that. If you wish to cancel your flight to Romania you have to cancel your flight to France, the fee for that is around half the price of the flight."

"What?!"

"You purchased the flights as a package deal. You can't cancel one flight from France to Romania without canceling your flight from Los Angeles to France."

"WHAT?!" I shrieked, my voice completely gone. I felt my heart begin racing as I struggled to come up with a plan. I was in Los Angeles, my mother's house was near San Francisco. I couldn't risk leaving the airport and not having a game plan of whether or not I would be turning around and flying back to my mother's house or spending a fortune to pay for a flight I had already paid for. "How much is the flight to France?" I risked, not willing to head home to mom's house and be defeated just yet.

"The plane boards in two hours..." the lady began typing furiously on the keyboard in front of her. "The seat you already paid for is already assigned to someone else...and the only other available seat is not in the economy seating. The cost of your flight will come to around...2500 dollars."

I nearly choked. "Let me get this straight," I sighed heavily, trying to comprehend the series of misfortunes that had been occurring recently in my life one after another. "I have to pay 500 USD to cancel my flight and then pay ANOTHER 2500 Dollars to secure the seat THAT I ALREADY BOUGHT to catch my flight into Italy on time?"

"Yes," she said flatly, completely fed-up with my crisis. "I recommend you go home and rebook another flight a month or two from now when the rates will be slightly cheaper."

Knowing that I could not afford to be jobless and homeless, wandering the streets of Los Angeles for the upcoming two months, especially when I had a job in Italy waiting for me, I strained to pull out my credit card from my wallet. I cringed as I slid the small piece of plastic-slash-heart-attack-inducing-death-contraption over to the woman.

She slid the card, securing my seat on Air France (I vowed to never fly with them again, something I've stayed true to nearly a decade later) and raised my unpaid bills and long overdue college debts another staggering 3,000 dollars.

Plus interest.

This job in Italy better be worth it...I thought to myself as I made my way towards the security gate.

I board the plane at the Los Angeles airport with a big wave of relief. Although I secretly dread the next twenty-six sum-mod hours I will be spending on three different airplanes and airports, a sense of calm resides within me. At this particular point in my life, I've been on enough airplanes to know how to handle myself. The strangest part is the fact that I never rode on a plane with another person I was familiar with. It seemed I was destined to see the world by myself, one way or another.

Always traveling solo has its advantages and disadvantages. Occasionally I would catch a glimpse of a couple in love—perhaps newlyweds? —and I would get a pang of loneliness and sadness inside my chest. Other times I would use my aloneness to my advantage and use it as an opportunity to make new friends from all over the world. It certainly helped to kill time if I engaged a stranger in an interesting conversation over the long stretch of my arduous flights.

More often than not I would be lucky enough to sit next to another solo traveler like me, however, the more I traveled the more I realized that the majority of these "single travelers" were all men. I had a nice conversation with an Australian man at the Dubai airport about how I focus too much on work and need to open up and allow men to approach me.

At the Sicily airport in Catania, I met an American Navy Soldier who had been stationed in Italy for a couple of years and was excited to travel back to the States and see his family and friends.

Flying into another country I was fortunate enough to sit next to an American man who had spent most of his childhood in Asia and was making his first family trip into an Arabic country. Turns out he was headed to Egypt for his first time. He gave me lots of interesting tips and advice about surviving Malaysia, whereas I was happy to give him some not so useful tips about Egypt, having spent one year of my life working there at a showjumping stable in Cairo.

My advice to him was as follows:

1. Remember when you're asking for a waiter and no one is answering you, just shout Ahmed or Mohamed and you have a 50% chance of guessing the waiter's name right.

2. Sunscreen! Alhamdulillah (Thanks to God)

3. The most amazing word ever invented in any language: Habibi! This Arabic word is used between a man and woman meaning: "my love" but if used between two males or two females the word is more like "my friend." Upon discovering this magical word, I proceeded to use it on nearly every horse, dog, or animal I encountered. Especially my Habibi, Asterix, my favorite horse in the stables during my stay.

4. If an Egyptian tells you he will meet you at 7 a.m. "Insha'Allah" (God Willing)...that means he's not coming and you can go ahead and give your lesson time to someone else.

But alas, this trip was to be another long and strenuous flight alone. Always alone, I thought to myself as I watched another happy Italian couple fondle each other on the bus taking me to my next terminal. The woman was pregnant and although the couple was rather plain looking I couldn't help but wonder. What would it be like to be them? Young, married, baby on the way... average clothes, not so much money, and not having seen much outside of Italy. Of course, this was all simple assumptions I based on after having spent years "people watching." Would you honestly give up your freedom, Krystal, just so you can have someone to love standing next to you? I watched the couple as they exchanged smiles and kisses and let out a deep breath.

Hell no, I grinned as I walked outside into the Italian air.

My first day on the job in Sicily and I was already stunned silent. The riding arena overlooked the Mediterranean Sea and in the distance, the mainland of Italy could be seen on the other side. My boss had been kind enough to send someone to pick me up from the airport as he was out for work. He was a lawyer and his Grand Prix Showjumping horses were simply a part-time hobby.

I was to be replacing a girl from Denmark, who I was introduced to upon my arrival. This blonde haired bombshell was literally, Danish Royalty, and her attitude, clothing, and style did nothing to counter-argue that fact. Stories about her family's Manor and lavish stables, not to mention her 30 thousand dollar designer saddle she "just had to have," filled my ears while I skipped yet another meal that day for not having enough pocket money to scrounge together to buy myself groceries. During the day the two of us split the horses to ride, making the work light enough, which I was thankful for.

I had realized somewhere in California between the full-length mirror and my mother's bathroom scale how much weight I had gained in the past several months. I knew when it started since I had fasted during Ramadan my digestive system and body didn't seem to quite understand what to do with food anymore. And the greasy, unhealthy food that was served daily to the customers and me while working in Romania hadn't helped much either.

Not to mention the Danish Royalty goddess across the room from me. She had the typical European build. She was petite in frame and stature, with thighs small enough for me to wrap my hand around. Working alongside European women for the past few months had done nothing to help my self-esteem. The women were all small, glamorous, chain smokers, skinny, fashionable, and trendy. Countless mornings and evenings of mine were spent sitting at the dinner table staring at the European Deities as I pondered how they could be so damn skinny and tiny while I watched them pick at their meager meals delicately.

I could starve myself for a lifetime and still never look as skinny and small as these women... I thought to myself as I helped myself to a third helping of food. Oh well if you can't join 'em, beat 'em! I wasn't exactly sure how I would go about "beating them" considering I was no competition for the fashionable European Divas. Even with their six-inch heels, they were miles beneath my shoulders and their outfits and outing wear was a far cry from my attire which was usually covered in sweat and dirt from the stables.

Of course, I tried my best to blend in, a chameleon that I am. In Belgium, I had lavished the day that I had splurged myself into buying a pair of high heel boots I had found on sale at the local market. Walking through rain and snow had never been more worth the journey. And in Egypt, I had prided myself on the "Egyptian Wear" sandals I had purchased on my last leg of the trip. Romania had gifted me with an afternoon of shopping followed by a well-earned splurge on a pair of furry boots to keep me warm that winter—and look cute while doing it I might add. Needless to say, I refused to spend my days in Italy, unfashionable, and shoeless.

The disappointment was in the air for me, however as I soon came to realize I wouldn't do much in the sense of sightseeing while on my short stay in Sicily. A horse show was approaching and as my boss decided I would be the one left alone at the stables—is there a reason why I'm always the one left alone?—while he and his groom took the bulk of the horses to the competition. For two long weeks, I would be tending to the horses and supervising the stables on my own.

The Danish girl was gone and shortly after, my boss, the groom, and horses followed suit leaving me once again alone in the world. For two weeks I struggled to push the wheelbarrow of muck and feces up the impossibly steep Sicilian slopes, rode my handful of horses each day, and—in my determination to lose as much weight as possible—I jogged each day. Whether it was late night jogging in place to music alone in my room or getting up at the crack of dawn to run laps around the arena or up and down the steep Sicilian hills.

Nearly ten pounds lighter and two weeks later, my boss returned from his competitions in Rome. My battle for the perfect body wouldn't stop there, however. I vowed to myself that I would no longer waste calories on food that wasn't at least worth the amount of weight I would gain from eating it, hence my newfound philosophy to not eat sweets or desserts unless it tastes so damn good it's worth the 3k run I would have to take afterward. Even if that meant simply taking one bite full of chocolate cake and refusing to finish the remainder on my plate because "it's good...it's just not THAT good..." (Much harder to do in Sicily where every dessert is THAT good.) I still don't know how I lost weight during my stay in Italy...

None of this mattered to me, however, that fateful day upon my arrival in Sicily. I wanted to impress my new boss with my riding skills, not my social status or blonde hair. And so I saddled up the first horse for me to try that day, a large beast of a horse known as Contender.

Determined to prove that I was a capable rider despite my added weight, after all, I had ridden OLYMPIC horses in BELGIUM and trained with a certified FEI Level II Coach in Egypt! I mounted onto Contender confidently. I eyed the big jumps in the arena, set for a staggering height of 1.65 meters. I sighed heavily as I wished for my chance to jump as big as that one day on horses such as Contender.

The arena was large and heavenly, the view of the Mediterranean soothing to me. I had been panicking and distressed since that moment I had been banned from Romania. Lost yet again and wondering where to go and what to do. Originally, I had intended on returning to Romania to work for Ionut after my 3-month ban had been lifted, however, due to finances I decided three months without work was too long to wait. The job in Italy had turned up as if on cue and I jumped at the chance while the opportunity was there.

I had thought I could simply work the job in Sicily for a couple of months as a temporary solution to my Romania disaster, however upon seeing the horses, the stables and after receiving my first month's salary—an amount that was triple than what I was making in Romania—I decided to make Italy my permanent solution. For now, at least.

Ionut had not been pleased to hear my news and the newfound decision to stay in Italy. Our conversation had not ended well, I reflected as I spurred Contender to life. My mind wandered to the short flight I had booked to Romania after my ban was lifted. I had agreed with Ionut and my new boss in Sicily that I would return to Romania for a week to get my things and help Ionut one last time with a large group of customers.

Contender dragged his feet on the arena floor lazily. His massive hooves shuffled across the sand with a clumsy, "thud." I had learned throughout the years how to properly warm up a horse, especially to the high level that was expected of these Grand Prix horses and I knew that if my boss were to see my horse moving like this on my first day of work he would be sure to regret hiring me. Without hesitation, I turned my whip upside down and gave him one crack on the hind to get this lazy horse's attention.

Contender put his head between his legs and with a force only a horse conditioned to jump a course of fences 1.65 meters in height, launched me from the saddle and his back in one buck. I flew like superman and landed face-first onto my belly a good two meters away. The fall had done nothing to hurt my body so much as it had my ego. I dusted myself off as my new Danish co-worker rushed to my aid. Upon seeing I was unhurt as I grabbed my reins and swung myself back in the saddle, she let out a laugh, "Don't worry, Contender got me on my first day of work too."

****

My first month in Sicily had been hard work. I spent six days a week riding 8 horses every day. Twenty pounds lighter and fitter, the riding became routine for me. I felt my muscles go through the motions as I exercised horse after horse. Although every horse has a different personality and style, I felt detached from the horses at this stable. These Grand Prix Show horses were machines. They had been bred, conditioned, and trained for jumping. They were professionals. They didn't need to be my buddy or friend. They wanted food, water, and work. Anything else was just annoying.

Even living in such a beautiful place as Sicily, I found myself become almost machine-like. I would walk down the hill into town to buy my groceries and eat my fresh minestrone soup, and occasionally enjoy a gelato, but as far as having a personal life and "fun" was concerned I was robotic. Bored with my daily work routine: wake up, ride horses, saddle horses, ride some more horses, saddle some more horses, ride some more horses, try not to fall off, ride some more, jog, eat, sleep, repeat...I was thankful for my day off.

It was my first day off after having worked in Sicily for a couple of months where I was spending the full day alone. My co-worker from Denmark had long since gone and my boss and the groom had left for the big competition in Rome. Six straight days of pushing wheelbarrows up hills that I swear had a ninety-degree angle, lifting hay bales, bucketing water, sweeping the aisles, bandaging and un-bandaging the horses' legs twice a day, multiplied by four legs per horse, and riding horses all day long had begun to wear on me. Needless to say, I was grateful for a half-day of rest (since I still had to feed the horses of course.)

Here's the thing: as tired and exhausted as my body was, I did not plan to sleep in on my one day of rest. Nope. "So what exactly was it you planned on doing?" You might ask.

I was going to take a jumping photo. Of me. Alone. On the beach. At sunrise. (And yes it had to be sunrise and not sunset because the beach was facing East.)

That's right. On my day of freedom I woke up an extra hour EARLIER, 4:30 am to be exact and scrambled to get dressed so I could walk down with my camera in hand in time to watch the sunrise. The only thing was...the sun started to rise without me. About halfway down the big hill, which I swear is at a ninety-degree angle, I realized I might not make it in time for my perfect camera shot. What's a girl to do?

I start running. Down the hill. A hill that I swear is at a ninety-degree angle...

At last, I make it to the beach, just in time for my perfect camera shot. I choose a decent spot on the beach for me to jump and begin toying with my camera. I settle it on a nearby rock and begin fiddling with the zoom, buttons, and timer. Then I proceeded to hit the button, race to the place I had picked on the beach, and try to time my jump just in time for the camera flash.

Three...two...one...now! Jump. Flash. Miss.

And again.

Three...two...one...Jump! Flash. Better...

And again.

Finally, I got the jump shot I had been hoping for. I smiled as I looked at my accomplishment on the camera film. Jumping photo in Italy: Check. Now to tell you the truth, I hadn't planned anything much further than that and when I looked at my watch it suddenly occurred to me that it was too early to go to a patisserie for early morning breakfast. What else was there to do other than head back home and sleep, right?

Wrong.

What I hadn't realized while I had been jumping up and down like a ridiculous fool trying to get a decent photo of myself and was thankful no one was around to see me, I had been wrong all along.

A small, local Italian fisherman had seen me. He had been fiddling with his boat nearby, preparing to launch when a stranger—me—had caught his eye. He approached me shyly, greeting me with a good morning in pure Italian. After attempting to converse with one another, we both realized very quickly 1) I didn't speak any Italian, and 2) He didn't speak any English.

Luckily for me the little Romanian I understood and spoke was similar to Italian and somehow I found myself able to understand the gist of what he was saying. Just don't ask me for details.

What would have been a lazy day spent inside my bed sleeping and feeding horses, somehow had turned into something else entirely when the man invited me to go fishing with him on his boat.

Now a normal person would most likely NEVER go with a strange man who 1) was alone 2) didn't speak or understand your language 3) was smelling strongly of fish and 4) offered you a ride on a small dinky boat to who-knows-where for who-knows-how-long.

"Andiamo!" I clapped cheerfully as I climbed into his boat. He handed me a pair of his spare fisherman gear, which turned out to be very useful while fishing, and I suited up. I'm one hundred percent sure I looked foolish for the second time that morning, but I didn't care. I was going fishing!

The man climbed into the boat and revved the engine. Before I knew it we were off, sailing our way further and further into the sea towards Messina. After an eternity of wave jumping and coasting casually across the sparkling blue waters, we slowed to a stop. Now I didn't know the name of my so-called fisherman friend, so I asked him as best I could. Imagine my delight when I found out his name, no it doesn't get any better than this, was Nemo.

Blonde girl that I am, I have never in my life gone fishing. Sure I had grown up most of my childhood living on the Sacramento River and sure I had spent every summer on the coast of Oregon with my grandparents and learned to go crabbing and sure I loved to eat fish...but still I had yet to test my skills in the art of fishing. And from the smell of things, I would have to wait a bit longer before I would try it out so instead, I was content to watch him.

He would put the bait on the line, throw the long string into the water and continue to unravel the long string that he attached to the boat. He would play with the string and move it this way and that but to no avail. For over an hour I watched as he moved from one spot to another attempting to catch a fish. Other fishermen came and flashed smiles and friendly waves before we would move to a different location and start again.

Still nothing.

To tell you the truth I was beginning to think my spontaneous adventure wouldn't be so adventurous. I also hadn't realized just how cold sitting out in the middle of the water was at 6 in the morning. I was shivering. I was wet. I was hungry. (Yes I was hungry for fish. Stupid fish. Just take the bloody bait already!) To top it all off the language barrier between me and the Italian man sitting across from me made for one very dull chit chat. The few times we attempted to speak to each other just ended with a few polite head nods—the universal signal meaning: I don't understand a word your saying but let me nod my head and politely pretend I do so you can shut up and we can sit in silence.

And just when I thought nothing interesting would ever happen, something interesting happened.

My Italian friend began pointing and waving and shouting in Italian. He kept repeating the word: "Delfino, delfino!" But of course, I didn't understand what he was excited about so I glanced casually in the direction he was pointing. I had my camera ready and began aiming it randomly, trying to figure out what the big hype was about. The man became very frustrated and tried even harder to grab my attention. His hands waved furiously and his sentences became too fast and lengthy for me to comprehend.

"The birds?" I said aloud as I attempted to take a photo of a seagull swooping into the water and catching a fish.

"No! No! Mama mia..."

And then I saw it.

"Dolphins!!!" I squealed. I had never in my life seen a dolphin, much less a pod of wild dolphins. The following ten minutes were the greatest ten minutes I could have asked for as I watched the wild dolphins swim right past our small fishing boat. "Baby dolphins!" I laughed as I took photo after photo. We watched the dolphins swim until we could see them no more in the distance. I was truly stunned.

After that, I returned home to the stables, fed the horses, ate some delicious Italian pastries, and caught up on some much-needed sleep.

****

I arrive at the smallest airport I had ever seen —which means a lot considering I've seen more than a hundred of them—only to discover that no one is waiting for me. I check and recheck my cell phone, brainstorming a plan of action. After several unsuccessful attempts at calling to speak to my Romanian boss, I am surprised to discover after speaking in broken Italian for the past several months that my slight Romanian kicks in as quickly as the phone picks up. It was the elderly cook and she didn't speak or understand a word of English. A brief and extremely broken conversation follows before I hang up my phone and yet again begin brainstorming my next move.

The stables are a three-hour drive so no point in trying to walk, especially with my suitcase. I search the contact list on my phone and begin calling various people, including my friend living a five-minute drive from the airport I currently stood. After failing to arrange any means and come up with any solution I check my pockets for the only cash I have in RON. (Romanian currency.)

"Taxi!" I wave to one of the drivers hoping that my 15 RON (about 5 USD) will be enough to get to the nearest hotel. Luckily for me, I got the only Romanian taxi driver not out to cheat me and although the fare was nearly 20 RON in total, I didn't have to walk or pay the difference.

"Multzumesk," I say to the boy, thanking him in Romanian as I struggle to remember the language. I walk inside the lobby of the hotel only to discover my ringing cell phone.

The cook had arranged for one of the customers to drive and pick me up to take me to the stables—don't ask me how I understood a word she said—and I was to wait where I was until they came. Instead of checking into a hotel room for the evening I seated myself in the lobby and played on the available computer.

For three hours.

My arrival at the stables was late in the evening and I was thankful for a hot shower and warm bed to sink into. I didn't know what was going to happen when I woke up the next morning to begin my final week of work at a job I had become so attached to.

It's all my boss's fault... I thought back to the day I tried to leave Romania only to be held by the police and charged a heavy fine. The angry officer made it a point to explain to me upwards of seventy times that I was illegally staying in his country (12 days longer than I was allowed) and that I was to be banned from the country of Romania for three months. This unexpected disaster had been my reason for working temporarily in Sicily, however the expensive fees and flight charges that followed after my blacklisting was more stress than I knew how to deal with.

Ultimately I had decided to take the job in Sicily as a more permanent solution to my financial problems since the salary in Romania was one fourth the pay. Of course, this decision had not suited my Romanian boss in the least. I didn't know if his absence from the stables this week was due to his anger towards me or because he truly was away on business, but I did know that for the next week I was running the entire stables and taking care of all the customers and decisions completely alone. Not an easy task considering I hadn't seen this stable, the horses, the customers, or this country for the past three months. I had to come back though since I had left all of my riding equipment and belongings here before I left. After all, I had no idea I would be forbidden to return as planned.

I crawled into bed and shut my eyes. Despite my normal tendencies to stay awake late thinking and planning, I fell asleep almost immediately. Hell, at this point I was a master in the art of "winging it" anyways...

My final week in Romania flew too fast for me to keep up. A large group of customers, my regulars from previous rides, had returned to wish me a final goodbye. It seemed everyone was just as sad as I was to have been banished from this wonderful country and I was thankful to have their support and help. Especially considering I still had a very large fine to pay and absolutely no clue as to how to go about paying it. With two of my customers' help, however, the issue was solved as they drove me to the police station to finalize everything.

"Krystaldo," my customers asked as I rode in the backseat of their car. It was a husband and wife couple. They were not very experienced in the saddle and a bit over-excited to gallop their horses at every second so I had spent lots of time giving private lessons to the couple. They both had a very different learning style, the husband being more logical and needing of theory and lectures and explanations whereas the woman was more hands-on. As a certified coach, I had learned long ago the best way to teach the different personalities—myself being a visual learner—and they had thrived on my lessons. In a short matter of time, I had transformed them into confident and capable riders.

"We have a favor to ask you," the man stated as he turned the wheel of the car up the windy road leading to the stables. I had never imagined my trip to the police station would be anything other than a friendly gesture so when I realized there was an ulterior motive my ears perked up.

"Sure, what is it?" I ventured.

"Well..." the wife looked to her husband. "We bought a horse."

"He is an excellent jumper!" The man piped. "He will jump 1.40 meters and never stop a fence. I'm serious this horse will crash into the jump before he would ever think about stopping."

"Oh?" My ears perked up more.

"The thing is..." the wife continued, her voice was more level and calm whereas her husband was as giddy as a schoolboy. "No one has jumped him in a very long time. He used to knock over the jumps a lot so the owners let him starve and become very skinny. We bought him for a very cheap price because nobody wanted him. They told us he was a crazy horse that should be sold for meat."

Flashbacks of my beloved Thunder, my first horse I ever owned as a late teen, came to my mind. "Then why did you two buy him?"

"Ever since I started taking those lessons with you back in December, I have been doing a lot of Dressage with him," the man said. "He is very fat and healthy now and I am working with him every day to make him calm and supple like what you taught me."

"I also ride him sometimes but I am a bit scared to ride him," the wife admitted. "He is too fast for me and I'm afraid I won't be able to stop him."

"So what's the favor?" I cut to the point. The stables were near and I wanted to wrap up our private discussion before we reached the others.

"You are flying back to Italy from Bucharest, no?"

I nodded my head. Bucharest was the Capital city of Romania and although I had never really explored the city myself, the majority of our customers, them included, came from Bucharest and filled my head with countless stories.

"Well we would like to give you a ride back to Bucharest with us and you can spend the night at our house before your flight. And we would like to take you to the stables to meet Live and ride him and if you would like to try to jump him so you can evaluate him for us and tell us what our future with him is like."

Although I usually never rode a horse for free, I was more than dying to be able to jump again. My work in Italy had not been going at all as originally promised, my boss failing to let me jump his horses. Of course, I wasn't about to admit that to them. Besides, they had just helped me to pay my fine to the government of Romania...

"Alright," I smiled. "I'm in. Just one question."

"Sure."

"What's your horse's name?"

The two smiled a big smile. They looked to each other lovingly as if what they were about to say would convince me further. Anyone who knew me, knew I was a firm believer in fate and destiny and karma and that things happen for a reason...

"Live for the Moment," they spoke simultaneously.

****

Excited for my return to his beloved stables and home in Sicily, my Italian boss couldn't control his eagerness as he welcomed me back. Ok, so he was more excited about the fact that he had just purchased a new Lori for the horses than he was in my return...but either way it was a day for celebration. (And in Italy any excuse was enough to make an ordinary day into a day for celebrating.)

My morning spent riding the gorgeous Grand

Prix horses in the outdoor arena overlooking the sparkling blue sea was only just the beginning as lunchtime rolled around. My only co-worker was the stable boy tending to the horses, so it didn't take long for our boss to load the two of us into the horse Lori in order for us to "celebrate" with a nice lunch down the hill inside the city.

"Krystal, Bella!" My boss, Mario, exclaimed to me as he took his place in the driver's seat. He started the ignition, marveling with dramatic gestures with his hands and arms at the miracle of his Lori as the engine roared to life. "You can start it so easily!" He gasped, kissing his fingers to his lips happily.

As we made the short drive down the hill Mario continued to tell me in great detail about his new beloved Lori. "It fits two horses in the back, so when we take the large six-horse Lori, you can drive this one," he flashed me a crooked smile as I thought about my Dusty Driver's License and my limited confidence at handling a manual car, let alone Lori.

Mario's smile grew larger as he shouted half in Italian and half in English. "It has a quiet-a engine, no? And look at these seats, so marvelous and comfortable, no? And look at the gears, so easy to shift," he bumped me with his elbow as the stable boy beside me rolled his eyes. Although the boy would have been a better choice to be the new designated Lori-driver in my opinion, I couldn't escape the fact that of the three of us packed inside the Lori, I was the only one other than my boss who hadn't failed his driving test for the fifth time in a row.

"And you see how the front of the vehicle is so small and low to the ground?" Mario took his eyes off the road yet again to look at me as he spoke. "This makes it feel as if you are driving a normal car and not a Lori!" I nodded my head, half in agreement as I tried desperately not to visualize what it would be like to be in the driver's seat, holding two horses in the back and attempting not to crash into the many tight turns, racing Vespa's and horn blowing cars.

"But there is one thing I don't like about this Lori." Mario's eyes suddenly grew very dark as he turned and faced me seriously.

My heart pounded in my chest as I tried to conjure up what possible detail his new fancy toy could be lacking that would cause him so much worry. "What's that?" I risked.

Mario sighed heavily as he looked at the container in his hand. "There is no cup holder for my beer," he shook his head as he simultaneously took a swig of beer from the can in his hands while eyeballing the road in front of him. "Can you hold this for me while I park the Lori?" He semi-asked me as he stuffed the empty can in my lap.

Only in Sicily…I thought to myself as I let out a hushed laugh.

The work had become gruesome for me. My daily routine of riding 8 Grand Prix Show Jumping horses around the beautiful arena over-looking the sea had become hell for me. Not only were these horses some of the most magnificent horses I had sat on…but I was absolutely forbidden to jump any of them. Instead, I watched as the Italian men, my boss included, jumped the horses over staggering heights. My boss, Mario had promised me on countless occasions to give me the opportunity to have a jumping lesson with him—hell at this point I would even be thrilled to walk over a pole on the ground—but his hot Italian temper always got the best of him and instead of jumping lessons I received curses, waving hands and flying spit.

Mario had flipped his lid the day he decided to curse me full volume. "Krystella! How can you expect to jump with the reins-a-twisted-alike-a-this?" I realized then that I would never be given the chance to jump any of his horses. After all, I hadn't even been the one to saddle the horse, his groom had. If that was all it took for him to make an excuse not to let me do what I had been training my whole life to do then enough was enough.

I drew the line and made my escape plan. A country far away called to me and I felt it in my bones that something greater was in store for me. I was tired of horses, to tell the truth. I was tired of getting shouted at for no reason. I was tired of my bosses and owners treating me like a joke. I was tired of people telling me the only reason I got as far as I did was because my hair was blonde, not because I was a capable rider.

It was time I started doing things MY WAY. After all, if I truly wanted to make it to the Olympics, I was going to have to get my own string of horses and start to train them to jump and go to the shows on my own. But I needed a place to start and money to buy my own horses. I had never been good at making plans, but I had always been one to follow my heart. Which is why what I did next came as no surprise: I emailed the owners of Live and took their job offer to return to Romania.

Having spent a short duration in Sicily—two and a half months to be exact—I was more than excited to have one last night out in Catania as a transition flight before making my way off into the unfamiliar territory at my new job in Romania.

A day of shopping in Italy had left me feeling like a rock star and I was more than eager to dawn my new well-deserved pair of Italian Prada shoes—don't ask how much it set me back, I had earned a treat for myself!—and outfit for a much needed night out.

That's right...I was taking myself on a date.

I didn't have time for men. After spending my days riding 6-8 horses, jumping, falling, ending up in hospitals, mending broken bones or getting stitches removed, constantly dealing with fatigue, stress, and pushing my body and mind beyond its physical and mental capabilities...let's just say at the end of the day I didn't have the energy to sit around and stare at my cell phone and wonder "why didn't he call me?!"

Now I wasn't always brave enough to take myself out on dates, mind you. In fact, back when I was enjoying being 18 and owning my very first truck and living in my very first apartment, I was terrified to go to a restaurant or to see a movie alone in the theaters. I thought people would judge me, stare at me, make fun of me, or what have you, and the fear of being criticized or laughed at had been too much for my teenage emotions to handle.

But all that had changed now. Now I was 22 years old, wiser, and more confident. I didn't need a man gawking at me to feel I was beautiful. I simply had to put on my new Prada shoes and pink sparkly top with some pink lip gloss and mascara to match and hit the road!

Italy was my romance movie. The moon was my love, the soft glowing street lamps my camera, the delicate cobblestone sidewalks my runway. Tall, dark Italian men approached me, some even slowing their vehicles down to attempt to catch my attention, but I wouldn't have any of it. I was already on a date, after all, and didn't want any disturbances or interruptions.

I walked for over an hour before settling on a quaint little restaurant tucked away by the harbor overlooking the glistening sea. I had been guided to the place by a local Italian—again another man trying to interfere with my date—but I waved him goodbye upon finding the adorable place to eat and sat at the table alone. I glanced at the menu—I already knew what I wanted—and ordered my favorite food in the entire world: Pizza. (And let me just say there is NOTHING better than an Italian pizza from Italy!)

I savored every delectable bite, imprinting the tastes into my palate memory. My senses were in complete paradise as I enjoyed the aromas of the food, the sights of the ocean at night, the sound of the rippling water, and the kiss of the warm breeze against my cheeks. After a peaceful calm had resided over me, I finally embarked on the long walk back to my hotel room. I was completely happy with my date, thinking I could easily spend a lifetime traveling the world solo chasing my love of horses.

Tales of an Equine Vet in the Kalahari Desert

BY MARIA BROS PONT

There I was, looking at a wound of almost ten by ten centimeters. Luckily it seemed not to have reached the thorax. There were splinters in the muscle, and flies were crowding on the coagulated blood. I was in the middle of the Kalahari Desert with no equipment, but my knowledge and two volunteers asking me to do something for the horse. My brain started to go a thousand miles an hour and I thought of everything that could be used to suture a wound. A clothesline would break easily and no one had a fishing line in the middle of the desert.

While I was deep in my thoughts and beginning to think that maybe I could put two or three pieces of wire (it was the only thing in that area) to at least reduce the wound, one of the volunteers offered me her dental floss. It seemed like a crazy idea, but it was indeed strong and durable and could work. I found a hypodermic needle big enough to pass a thread through it. Well, there I was, in the middle of the desert, about to suture a horse without sedation, with a hypodermic needle and dental floss. I was not sure if the horse would allow me to do it, without using any tranquilizer, but I was willing to try. Even risking my life.

One of the volunteers put the twitch on the horse, and I began to disinfect the wound, with some products that I had never seen in my life. I could not find anything to shave the skin around the wound...

Nothing was hygienic, but I had to keep the flies from laying eggs in the wound and avoid septicity. After disinfecting the thread and passing it through the needle, the serious part began. I advised everyone present to be alert to the horse's reaction. I took the piece of skin where I was going to put the needle first, with my hands and punctured. I pulled away quickly, I think it is a reflex I have acquired from treating horses for a long time, but the horse did not flinch. I sighed, and the two volunteers who helped me, smiled. I told them not to relax, there was a lot of work ahead, we would see how he would react to the next puncture.

The needle was still stuck there, I picked up the piece of skin that was hanging, as close to the needle as possible and punctured again. The horse continued as if nothing had happened. I took out the needle and gave it to one of the girls, so she could start to pass another thread through it, while I tied the knot. With the first suture in place, I calculated how many points I would need, it would be a few, possibly around twenty minutes of work. A miserable twenty minutes they would be.

There was no way to go fast because the dental floss was defiant and did not want to go through the eye of the needle easily. The whole process must have taken us about two hours, we gave the horse a few minutes of rest from the twitch now and then, but we never stopped. Finally, the wound was well sutured and I was able to leave a hole to drain and wash. Luckily, there was a bottle of antibiotic and anti-inflammatory drugs in the stables closet, and we were able to administer it. It was just another day in the Kalahari Desert. I had been in Namibia only for a week and already had to stitch up a horse with dental floss. *What else is waiting for me out here in the coming six weeks?* I wondered, with a mix of concern and excitement.

I had decided to come to Namibia as a volunteer because I love Africa with its animals and different cultures. In addition, I was able to combine it with my great passion, horses. Although I am already fully dedicated to horses, since I am an equine veterinarian, enrolling as a volunteer to guide horse safaris, seemed like a dream job. Namibia is a desert country. There are few cities and towns and the distances from one place to another, are enormous. When I got the opportunity to volunteer, I knew little about Namibia and the Kalahari, but it all sounded so exciting that I did not think about it twice. And I did not regret it.

The Kalahari is considered a semi-arid desert with reddish, infertile soil. Due to a bad drought which had gripped Namibia for several years, it had become a hostile place for animals who—without human help—only have the choice to migrate or die. The lodge I stayed in, provided extra food for the wild animals surrounding it so that they could continue to live in the area without the threat of starvation. Still, life here for both humans and animals was tough.

One day, while I was cleaning the stalls, one of the San men (the san is a local tribe) who worked as a maintenance guy, asked me to help him. They were relocating a building inside the stable compound and were at that moment taking out the floor tiles. I came to help them, trying to lift a single tile which was so heavy, that I could not pick it up. The five guys around me were clearly having some fun at my expense, and

I felt like the weakest person on Earth, unable to do the same work as them. I had wanted to show them that women were as strong as men and I completely failed. But I was not going to quit that fast and continued the work.

When I was about to move the second tile, a scorpion came out from under the tiles. I freaked out and dropped the tile again. One of the maintenance guys tried to kill the scorpion, but then the one that asked before for help stopped him and said they were animals from the desert and they did not harm the san people. He took the scorpion with his hands, started petting it, and showed it to me.

"I am not a San, so it's better for me to stay away from that animal," I said to him.

I was still talking with him when two baby scorpions came out from under the tiles that another guy was moving. There was a whole scorpion family under those tiles. It was the same building in which a family with a small child had been living.

The san man was not yet finished. He picked up another large scorpion and let it climb onto his clothes! All the time the man remained calm. At the moment the scorpion reached his neck, he took it and started caressing it. This scorpion looked more aggressive than the other ones.

However, that was not a problem for the san man, he put one of his hands under his armpit, and then pet the scorpion with that same hand. He did that several times, even with a piece of straw. He put the piece of straw under his armpit, then touched the scorpion with it. I had no clue, what was going on, but that scorpion kind of fell asleep. I was absolutely astonished; it was definitely the most bizarre thing I have ever seen. I was still keeping an eye on the old man, to make sure no scorpion was left inside the stables, but the san man freed all of them outside at a certain distance from the stable. Although he said scorpions do not hurt san people, the other men did not touch any scorpion and they were trying to kill them, as we would kill cockroaches. For what I knew, he was one of the oldest san men and probably one of the few who knew how to survive in the desert.

I was always around san or other native Namibian people. The workers' kids came to help and play with me and the horses. Some days I had only one kid, other days I had four or even more kids. I clearly remember the day I had a dozen kids or so. I did not understand why they came all together. They were of different ages, and although most of them spoke English, between them they spoke their native language, so

I could not understand what was going on. I was explaining to some children how to brush a horse when at the same time a few of them were putting a halter on one of the other horses, while others were spooking a horse that was loose in the stables.

I was shocked, all those barefoot kids, screaming and treating the horses as if they were toys, that could not end well! I shouted at the kids who chased the loose horse around while trying at the same time to keep an eye on the ones brushing and haltering the horses. Finally, a woman came, shouting something in an incomprehensible language and all the children disappeared, as if by magic. I could not make a disappearance so quickly, surely because I did not know what was coming. The women shouted at me for letting the children get close to the horses.

"I was just trying to show them something new and have a good time," I stammered, trying to explain my reasoning for inviting them inside. "But then it just got out of control very quickly!"

The woman frowned and did not quite agree, and after saying a few disapproving words to me, left. That was a very awkward moment. I hoped I would not find myself in that situation again.

Luckily, the normal thing was that only a few children came. There was a kid who came every day and he helped me a lot. I could tell that kid loved horses. I taught him to put on halters, brush the horses, and put the tack on. At the end of the morning, I let him ride an easy horse, and I taught him the basics. After ten days or so, the kid had to leave, he was moving to another lodge with his father. He told me, he wanted to be a cowboy when he was older. I felt very sorry that I could not teach him anything else, but I hoped he would find a good place where he could learn more.

After he left, I had two girls and one little boy who came every day. It was harder with them because they were younger and full of energy! But still, I tried my best to teach them something and make their school vacations a little bit less boring. Although sometimes I had to send them home, because they became too unruly, they were good kids.

The Namibian kids were all amazing; they could speak so many languages! At the very minimum, they could speak three languages: their native language, Afrikaans and English. But some of them also spoke Portuguese and several other native languages. Their lives were quite hard. Many lived with their grandparents because their parents worked away from home and they only saw them during their vacations. Those who could all live together as a family stayed in very simple houses and I wondered how they managed to go to school since they lived in the middle of the desert.

Although my job was to do the safari tours and take care of the horses, I felt very happy to teach those kids something different, and give them the chance to ride a horse. The most important thing for me was to teach them empathy towards the animals.

And yes, I also did my job as an equestrian guide on safaris! Luckily, it was low season, and I was able to enjoy many trails through the desert on my own, finding new routes and discovering the area. Every day in the morning or at dusk, when it was cooler, I saddled a horse and rode out. Sometimes there were guests with me, other times I was accompanied by volunteers but often, it was just me and my horse.

One day, I decided to try the horse no one wanted to ride because he was "naughty." I thought he would buck or do something similar, but they told me that he never bucked, he was just "naughty." When someone does not clarify *why,* you should perhaps have more caution than I had. But, never mind, I rode the horse in the small arena we had behind the stables. I needed to know what naughty meant.

I realized the horse was fast and he was hard to stop, but other than that, he was a very nice horse. I could not understand why everyone found him so difficult. In the desert, if you cannot stop a horse, you face it towards a dune, and the fatigue of the climb in the sand will cause it to slow down eventually. I kept thinking that there was something else wrong because this horse did not seem so excessively "naughty."

The next day I went trail-riding with a few volunteers and I took the "naughty" horse. That day I truly understood why he was considered to be so. Just leaving, he reared up twice, when I tightened the reins. So, I did not touch his mouth and was very soft with him, and it seemed to work for the time being. After ten minutes of riding, he started sneezing all the time and pawing with the front limbs. It was as if something had gotten into his nose and he was trying to get it out. I was concerned, maybe some kind of insect or even a scorpion had stung him or was stuck in his nose and I hadn't noticed!

I expected the worst. I took the bridle off, I cleaned his nostrils I did everything I could, but he still did the same thing. At that point I thought it was too late, maybe something neurological was going on with him. I turned him back to the stables, worrying that the horse was going to die here and now, in the middle of nowhere, and that I would not be able to get any kind of help. As we went back to the stable, he started trotting and cantering. Well, he looked fine for the moment, so maybe we could reach the stables and I could treat him there or at least, let him rest in peace.

We arrived at the stables and I jumped from the saddle, the moment I saw the stable gate. I took the saddle and the bridle off, as fast as I could. I did not care; I threw everything on the ground and left him alone in the middle of the stables to see what was going to happen. He had a bucket of water next to him, but he did not drink. He lowered his head and he started to pick some hay that was on the ground. I said to myself, ok, let's make sure he is not having a heat stroke. I brought him close to the water and I wet his mouth and his head.

Nothing.

I looked at his gums and did a quick physical. He was absolutely fine! At that moment I realized he was the smartest horse I had ever met. He had tricked me!

I was happy that he was fine and I had found a smart mind to work with. I brought him to the round pen and worked him on the lunge line, trying to make him understand that he could not do that with me again. Later I told one of the other guides what had happened and he just shrugged and told me that the horse loved to paw and that he was naughty.

Naturally, there came the day, we had to use him again for riding when we had a large group and needed all our horses. On those trails, I had to take my "naughty" horse, because nobody liked him, and I did not care that much. He always behaved quite well when working and just did some pawing now and then. I think, at that point, we knew and took care of each other. I was very gentle with him, and although usually we had to stay at the end of the group, he was quite patient. One time I even had to pony another horse, and he did his job without any nonsense. He was just a very sensitive and demanding horse, but if you could understand him, he would do what he had to do. It wasn't just that he liked to paw, it was his way of communicating with his riders, saying that something bothered him excessively.

On another ride, we found a group of giraffes who lived on the property close to us. The giraffes were hard to see on the horse safaris because they usually stayed far from the stables. It was a pity that the group was quite inexperienced, so we could not gallop alongside them, a life-long dream of mine. But that made me go every morning when I had no one with me, to find the giraffes.

I wanted to gallop with them so much! Every day at dusk, I would ask the game-drive guides where they had seen the giraffes. According to what they told me, the next morning I was going through the area where they had been sighted the evening before. I was a bit obsessed with them, but then I enjoyed every ride, giraffes, or no giraffes.

I remember one day doing a race with one of the working cars. I won the race, but I think it was because the guy in the car got scared of seeing me galloping that fast, so close to the car on a narrow sand road. But the horses were bomb proof, you could do almost everything you could imagine with them.

Another time, I went far from the typical trail riding routes and found a group of wildebeest eating alfalfa in one of the feeding stations. Usually, the antelopes would start running when they saw us, but these did not care. I approached them very slowly, as I did not want to provoke a stampede. We inched closer and finally my horse was eating alfalfa together with the antelopes. I really enjoyed the moment, despite being a little tense. It was not yet too hot and we were in the shade of a tree. I heard the animals chewing while the time flew away. I felt like a thirsty adventurer who had discovered a fresh spring.

I was never bored at the lodge. One day, one of the workers came back with an orphaned baby oryx. He still had the placenta attached to him and nobody knew what happened to his mother. I thought the baby was going to die, without colostrum and in the middle of the desert. We started giving unpasteurized cow milk, as we did with the two other baby oryxes we had. Then I waited to see what would happen. The baby oryx did great the first days. Although we had to feed the three babies several times during the day and at night, it was a very satisfying job. The baby oryxes were the sweetest animals in the lodge. But then what I feared, happened. The little oryx, when he was around two weeks old, stopped drinking milk, and became very lethargic.

The workers and volunteers asked me again to do something for him, but I told them, that I had never dealt with antelopes. How was I supposed to treat a baby oryx? I could not use my knowledge, as I did with the injured horse, because I did not know about antelope, let alone a sick antelope. I was again absorbed in my thoughts when I finally summoned up my courage and told them that I would treat him like a foal.

Everyone was happy, although I knew, that even if I treated him like a foal, what did I have to treat him with? There were still some medicines in the stables and since he was a baby, he would not need much. I also thought, that if he did not drink, I could find a hose to intubate him and pass the milk directly to his stomach. With those ideas in mind and the possibility that I could do something, I started doing a physical exam. I looked at the mucosa, obviously all pigmented, I suppose it was normal in antelope, but that did not give me any information. The mucous membranes were very dry so I could deduce that he was dehydrated. I looked at the conjunctiva of the eyes and it looked pink, the normal color. Since I did not have a stethoscope, I could not auscultate the heart, the lungs nor the intestines. I placed my hand on top of the heart (just behind the elbow) and started counting its beats. Unfortunately, he had a very high heart rate and I did not know what the normal heart rate of a baby antelope was, I could not compare it to a foal, because the oryx was four times smaller.

So far, I had very little information about what was happening to him. I took the temperature and it was 39.5°C. The normal temperature for a foal is up to 38.5°C, so I chose that temperature as a reference. Summing it up, I had a dehydrated animal with a fever and a little cough in front of me. I was concerned about aspiration pneumonia, quite typical in bottle-fed animals, plus he did not have good immunity due to the lack of colostrum when he was born. I started treating him with a very small dose of antibiotics and anti-inflammatories, and I told them to feed the baby with cold instead of warm milk, to help reduce the fever. The temperature outside every day was around 35 to 40°C, so it was imperative to do everything to cool down the baby. If after two hours he did not want to drink, the next step was going to be to find a hose and intubate him. But that little oryx proved again that he was a warrior! That same night he was already drinking milk again. We still treated him with antibiotics, and I was going to check him for a fever every day.

As the days went by, it was a bigger challenge to take his temperature and give him the daily injections. Fortunately, there were two of us and we tricked him with the milk and held him down. On the third day, we were not even considering taking his temperature, he was too wild. Some days I had to inject him alone. It was me, against a small oryx of about 10 kg, who when he noticed that I was taking his legs to knock him down, fought with all his strength against me. When I had succeeded in pushing him down, I would put one knee against his neck and I would put the other leg half stretched on top of his body, trying to control him. Putting the injection, I had to withdraw my knee a little bit from the neck and with my free hand, extend his head well and hold it against the ground. I had a space of about two centimeters to put the needle in a place other than the vertebrae. The moment I injected the needle, he would turn into a crazy baby oryx. I only had to administer about 1 ml of penicillin, but it seemed like an impossible mission. I don't even know how I managed to do it. That little guy gave me the hardest time.

One day, they also brought a sick adult oryx. He could not walk, he was just lying down sternal, and not eating nor drinking. I came to see what I could do, after the success with the baby oryx and the dental floss horse, I was optimistic. Although the oryx was in pretty bad shape, each time we tried to approach with hay or water, he would try to hit us with his horns. A big problem with adult wild animals is that you cannot restrain them for treatment very long, because they can die a few hours later from the stress. It was a very complicated situation. We tried grabbing his horns to have control and see if I could inject at least something. Three people were grabbing the horns, and that animal was fighting as if we were lions. Finally, we left him alone, to see if he just needed some water or food. The next day we found him dead. It was very sad, but as a vet, the first lesson you learn is that you cannot save all animals.

There was a period when I was the only volunteer in the horse section. Only two native workers came to help me during those days. The cleaning part was hard, but working with the horses was amazing. It was low season, so we did not have a lot of horse rides with tourists. I had plenty of time to do my horseback trails around the property, enjoy the swimming pool, and see lots of wild animals. I was only allowed to go to the pool when there were hardly any guests. Luckily, I had weeks where I could go almost every day before lunch. While I was taking a swim, I was able to see one of the feeding posts. I could see ostriches, kudus, elands, oryxes, donkeys, lots of springboks, and guinea fowls. It was such a relaxing and enjoyable moment. I leaned against the edge of the pool and was watching the animals eat and drink. It was so peaceful. The warm sun roasting my skin, while my body was soaking cool and my eyes looking at that heavenly landscape. It was pure bliss. Those moments made me understand the love that Karen Blixen, writer of the book *Out of Africa*, had for the African continent.

I not only got the opportunity to enjoy the animals from a distance. I was able to be close to them, sometimes very close. On two occasions, I had the opportunity to help with feeding the rhinos and antelope which were roaming around the property. Because of the drought, the workers had to make sure that every day, all animals had enough food to survive, and of course, the rhinos ate a lot! There were two rhinos and I remember watching them from the back of the pickup. They made funny noises while eating, and it was very difficult for them with that big mouth and those lips to carefully select the alfalfa pellets and the hay branches, unlike the way horses do. As a vet, I could only think of the large amount of sand they were ingesting, but as an animal lover, I found it fascinating. Sometimes the rhinos were so close, they rubbed their skins together and it sounded like they were rubbing two pieces of sandpaper.

On several occasions, I had the opportunity to feed cheetahs, which was an indescribable experience. I was asked to help with the cheetah feeding, although I probably did not help that much, however, it was so amazing to be so close to these animals. The cheetahs were separated, in a big enclosure on the property, so they did not attack anybody. We fed the cheetahs from a bowl which we were holding with one of our hands, while with the other one, we were stroking them on their heads, and cleaning their eyes and ears.

The younger cheetahs were still quite wild, and you had to be very careful when feeding them. But the older ones were nice, and I could get very close while feeding them. I remember that while they were eating, they almost looked like hungry big cats and nothing else, but by the time they finished, even the oldest ones would always look up and fixate their eyes on yours. Then they would scream and leave. Although I fed them repeatedly, each time a pair of those eyes made contact with mine, I noticed how my blood ran cold and I got goosebumps. They told me that this was their way of thanking me. For me, it was their way of saying, "Today, I spare your life."

Another wild animal whom I got very close to, sometimes even too close, was the eland (also a type of antelope). They were expert ninjas, sneaking into the stables for food and they even knew how to open the door of the feed room! The youngest, was able to slip through the hole that was near the gate, which had been made in a way, that only people could pass. The first time I saw how he entered, I was amazed! First, he carefully passed his head with his horns, and then, little by little, one leg after another, he even entered a little diagonally, so that his hip did not get stuck. He had it all calculated!

The oldest one was not afraid of horses, and he threw them out and stole their food. Every time I saw them sneak into the stables, I would run after them shouting, so they would leave. They were my eternal enemies during my stay at the lodge.

I continued with my morning rides and finally, one day, when I was going back to the stables, it happened.

Giraffes!

I could not believe it! At first, I saw only one. That was strange, usually, they were all going together, in a big group, but then behind the one I saw, came the rest.

My horse, the nicest horse for an experienced rider we had in the stable, was a little bit concerned about those long-necked grass-eaters, but when I nudged him into a canter, he went full speed! I was recording the whole thing with my cellphone in one hand, while with the other one, I was trying to not lose control of the horse. The giraffes started running and it was more of a chase than the happy galloping I had in my mind. Still, I was so happy and it was pure adrenaline. I could not hear the giraffes galloping, I just heard my horse's breathing and the wind. The sand muffled the noise from my horse's hooves. The speed was such, that tears streamed from my eyes. I climbed up a dune, and that was where my "hunt" ended. The giraffes looked at me suspiciously. My horse was still nervous, he wanted to continue galloping. I patted him, to calm him down. It was time to go back.

Besides riding on the trails, the wounded animals were still one of my daily chores. All the fences were made with wire and every week there was a new wound to be treated. I remembered the day I realized all the horses' ears were full of ticks. Thankfully I had a product ready to kill the ticks. I guess you can imagine "the fun" I had, spraying those ears, plus the paranoid fear that at least one of those ticks might fall inside my shirt.

On another occasion, I had two horses who came down with acute colic. The pain killer medication I gave, did not have any effect. Luckily, this time I could contact a local vet and he came to treat both of them. The next morning, one horse was well, but the other horse, actually a pony, was still the same. Additionally, some other horses started having diarrhea. But I was more worried about the pony. Every day I was checking on him, injecting pain killers and making special soft food for him with the alfalfa leaves. After four days of being sick, everybody could tell how much weight he had lost. He was also not passing any manure at all. I told the managers that I thought he was going to die. But then, little by little, he started eating a bit more, and I found some small fecal balls in his stall. After a week, he was a normal pony again. The diarrhea problem, took about two to three days for each horse to get over. Almost all horses acquired it eventually. It seemed that something contagious went around. But thankfully, all of them survived. After all, they were Kalaharian animals—big fighters!

At the end of my days as a volunteer at the lodge, while I was resting in my room, two volunteers came to tell me that there was a foal in the baby oryx enclosure. Now before continuing the story, I must tell you about the amazing room I was living in. It had a bed covered by a mosquito net, a couch, two working tables, and a huge bathroom. Everything was decorated with African motifs, and I had the comfort of air-conditioning.

Going back to the story, I first thought it was a joke. There were only male horses, so no chance a foal could have been born. They insisted, however, so I finally agreed to go, although I was sure, they were mistaken in some way. We arrived at the baby oryx enclosure, and all the babies were in a corner scared and in the middle was an overo-colored foal, with a brown and a blue eye, running here and there, confused and frightened.

I was astonished. How was that possible? In the same moment, I saw a few spots of blood on his legs (not his blood) and he had a swollen eye. He was lost and confused and I immediately felt pity for him. We took him to the stables because the baby oryxes were in a real panic about him, and I also thought it was better for the foal to be around horses so he would calm down. We put him in the pony enclosure, with the ponies left outside, so the foal could relax. We washed his legs and his injured eye because he could barely open it. The foal was probably around three months old, so we gave him hay and water.

During dinner time, I started my investigation about the foal. They told me he had come with the dead animals they used to feed the cheetahs. His mother had been in bad shape, so it was decided to put her down and use the meat for the animals and the baby was brought to us. I got angry upon hearing that they had killed the mother. Even though she might have been in bad shape, we surely could have done something for her. I was very pissed for several days. I guess after a while, I understood that in countries where people starve every day, some things are simpler and some resources cannot be spent on a sick animal. At least, somebody cared about the baby foal and brought it to the stables.

The next morning, the foal was introduced to the ponies. One of the ponies was very interested and even dangerous for the foal, another one did not care at all and the last one, the oldest one, adopted him. We kept a close eye on how things went, but it was good for the foal to be around horses and learn to live in the group. His eye was healing and after a few days, the sad, terrified foal we met in the baby oryx enclosure, was happy and settled with his new companions.

On my last ride, before leaving, I found the giraffes again. They looked at me and it was like a signal that I could make peace, after the chase I gave them the last time. I approached them very carefully and went as close as I could. It was magical. The group comprised of two baby animals, a teenager, and an adult. The rest of them were probably around, eating somewhere nearby.

I was finally together with the majestic creatures I had been dreaming about all this time. They were there with me, so close that I could see their features clearly and watch them eating leaves from the thorn trees with their blue tongues. I spent a long time just being there with them, observing them, and feeling the magic that was Africa. Time froze still as I watched how they lived peacefully in the Kalahari Desert.

Randolph County

BY SARAH MURPHY

My finger was broken. My horse lay three and a half feet below me, sprawled flat out in knee-deep mud. I asked myself for the millionth time: how did I get here?

****

My grandfather was a logger in rural Pennsylvania and from what I've been told in family lore he used horses to pull trees loose when he was just starting as a man in the timber business. This was all before the sawmill where my mom once spent her summers and her twin sister lost the tip of her thumb.

Before the faded, grainy picture of him in faded jeans, the ubiquitous countryman's plaid shirt with pearl buttons and shit-kicker cowboy boots. The one where I'm sure I was on a pony for one of my first times, a shaggy little Shetland thing in child size overalls and a blunt little bob (short haircut). I couldn't have been more than three at the time and that moment had clearly sealed my fate forever on.

He used to take us on big family rides. Ten or more horses deep, we would cover the coarse bristled fields like some Western posse, a Hatfield, or a McCoy. We covered the land looking for a place to high line the horses while we slept in the open; my young eyes staring up at the stars searching for a sign of my place amongst them.

This was many horses before the one that would be a touchstone for almost twenty years of my life. Rob Roy, once deeply dappled silver, whose muscles became stringier every year, whose coat had graciously slid into the flea-bitten one he sported now. Who came through three winters with a little more rib every time.

Many years beyond his noble fox hunts in the rolling hills of Virginia we would come to this place, of steep rugged mountains sliding down on hocks precariously to reach a bottom gulley we would only have to turn around and climb again. Angles and turns better left to a protractor than a horse and woman laden with gear and a mission that seemed impossible.

A "natural gas" pipeline was coming through. A 42" structure to be buried for 600 miles through much of Appalachia, to the coast, into the swamp and through the land that I had grown up in and loved for most of my adult life.

The mountains were my heart, my home, steeper and more foreign here but with a pulse that I recognized. A shift that had been born eons ago when land met the land and pushed itself towards the sky.

It had already been months to reach this precipice. We'd come so far already, hundreds of miles to the terminus. The inconsequential beginning from near a little country church and nestled into wet little marshes. I'd already made acquaintance with pipe-liners, head of security, resistance fighters, West Virginians so tied to their lands they couldn't tell you where it ended and they began.

We'd already narrowly missed death daily. Coming out of belly-deep mud to receive a trespassing charge from the gas company responsible for the destruction we'd already seen. I'd already watched his eyes flicker as he fought to free himself yet continued sinking, legs wedged between underlying rocks as he'd thrashed back and forth in his attempts to extricate himself and keep his nostrils from breathing in the water that continued to run down the sluice. Only the backhoe, once started and throttled by the workers who had come to our aid gave him the muster for the final push to set himself free. It was only by the grace of God he was gifted swollen legs streaming minimal blood from nicks and cuts gained during his struggle.

My thanks had carried in the necessary ways, praying for a clearer vision of whether we should risk the ultimate sacrifice, skirting danger to continue, or if we should throw in the towel as had been suggested by countless mouths and pack up and head on home.

You always think you know exactly what to fear not knowing the things you don't fear at all might ultimately be your undoing. I had been warned about the mud season but had shrugged it off lightly; I knew red clay, the tacky viscousness of bricks, and potter's wheels. This was another beast, pushed and mauled into steep embankments that gave an illusion of firmness but lay in wait to suck off boots and bring you to your knees.

We'd left our hosts the prior morning in high spirits, an extra day of rest because an impenetrable mist had rolled in obscuring roadways traveled by coal trucks roaring into the day and night. We had seen Maple syrup farmers, a musician, and a writer who's property boasted cool pools that they moved trout into as they grew from darting minnows into fat, speckled things cutting the surface of the water and circling restlessly onto a dinner plate.

The roads are winding, bending, stretching to make space, and wrap themselves around an unforgiving topography that doesn't bend well to man's hands. We passed the coal company, it's mouth spitting out the trucks with regular frequency, who refused to slow down and make allowances for no shoulder and a live animal who's PTSD from a logging truck in year's past made him skeptical of large machines at best, blindly terrified at worst.

As the coal trucks dropped the would-be diamonds along the side of the road, everything was covered in a fine, black dust that made it hard to breathe, even in the open. We'd railed against this extractive industry years before and part of me was surprised to see it alive and well carrying out its business as usual even as the markets declined and new technologies surged to take its place.

Home and all the things I loved seemed so far away but I could feel it pushing me, yet pulling me back towards it in every step. I consulted the map that defined our route. Five miles to each side of the pipeline's gnarled and twisted route with access roads were defined in black. The pipeline itself was a blazing red trail we could no longer directly follow with the yellow paper given to us stating as much from our previous accident falling off the right of way.

The coal trucks kept coming, one after the next, after the next. Some drivers more polite than others, some almost daring a game of chicken to see how close they could come to us then screaming out the window when Rob Roy's shoes sparked across the asphalt, hind end hinging both towards and away from the gleaming metal, bouncing off of guard rails.

The hardest part is the way your nerves feel when your whole self is present, both through good and bad. The way your veins pump blood and your heart pounds. Adrenaline is a drug that will short-circuit all the systems, more and more flooding receptors, and endings until they fray and skitter and scatter across your skin.

The map showed an access road, a relief from what already felt like hours of an onslaught. So we turned, not a true road but a road for us on two feet and four. The thing about long-distance travels, end epic journeys, and adventures is the not knowing, how you can use every clue and sign and tool and trick to try to carry you in the correct direction but never really knowing which point A leads to B and which way the winds might blow or if they'll even turn your way at all.

But this was peace, our reward for pushing on through the uncertainty. We'd stumbled across an old railway line from who knows when. It's skeleton of a wooden frame succumbing to the woods once more as the beams rotted beneath our feet. We pushed our way forwards, bewitched by beaver dams and waterfalls, weaving over and under and around long fallen logs.

It was every fairy tale told to children in the semi-darkness before the haziness of sleep overtakes them. Pristine and pure it belied the blackness that surrounded it in shades of verdant green and crystal clear waters plunging itself over and over each ledge, pool, and eddy.

You don't realize you're not breathing until you can. The way your diaphragm clenches tight until it can uncoil again and your feet touch ground repeating a prayer to the soil over and over. This is why we came. This is what we were defending, this true power that is free and wild and beyond ourselves.

We passed a coal tipple, lost a sweatshirt in a river crossing. Little marks of time passing and things seen. Dead deer along the now gravel road that began climbing, the accent revealing itself in both our breathing. We kept seeing and kept feeling until we could no more. Our bodies stretched to the limit of what a day could both bring and take from us.

I found a cut beside a creek, the wind had begun to kick up whether spurring us on or objecting remained to be seen. There was grass for the boy, his appetite insatiable at night. My tent was easy to set up, the fire to make much harder. Each star began to make itself known as the dark slid in deeper and deeper. Once again I fell asleep to the sound of the big grey Goliath taking his fill as the winds tore through the hillsides.

Daybreak struck again as I began the tedious tasks to pack up camp. Every morning after camping an inventory of what goes where. It's during the tacking that the mind begins to both race and calm itself. Running through all the possibilities of what could go right and wrong as those inner workings seek to both soothe themselves and continue to rile itself up to racing speed. It's the repetition of saddle pads, saddle, latigo, saddlebags that begins to steady its meanderings.

The maps had shown only two short miles from the point we were at to where we wanted to be. Turkey Bone Road had become a mantra from many mouths; a place we'd passed before which I could catch my bearings and senses. A sunny Sunday in late fall and the ground had thawed again. It had been on a repetitious pattern of freezing, thawing, and freezing again in the wintry mountain mixes of sleet, snow, and rain. It was this perfect combination that encouraged the encroachment of mud.

We passed the bottom of a logging cut, their mighty machines silent in respect of the day of rest. We were in God's country still but what had seemed like a slice of heaven would become hell today, but I didn't know that yet as we began the ascent, slipping and sliding our way to the top of the small mountain.

The thing about this kind of mud is unlike water, you can't see the bottom. While one part was shallow, the other would be deep and leading to the edge of the mountainside, a dare to slide and be gone to the beyond. I stayed to the higher ground, wary after our previous experience. While once before we had been rescued by two walkie-talkie wielding flaggers who ran to our aid and radioed others, here there was no one but he and I and the crows and birds wheeling overhead in the cloudless heavens.

The sun beat down, peeling layers of clothes, the resistance dragging my legs in slow motion. Ladened with backpacks and bags, steps grew even slower and more uncertain. Time was becoming as sticky and oozing as the mud until it almost stopped completely.

I'd taken Rob Roy to even higher ground to the rim crusted edge of the sludge until it became just a sliver that barely contained our feet. He had a bad habit of rushing up behind me when nervous, I turned around to yell at him and wave my arms to back his hot breath off the back of my neck and to keep his hooves from clipping the backs of my boots when the ground gave way. I watched his eyes briefly roll back wide in his broad head as he toppled over the side, the lead rope in my hand catching my finger as all his weight went down multiplied by velocity and height.

What happened was both so fast and so slow, it knocked the wind out of him. He lay completely still while pain seared through my hand. I hardly thought about it as I jumped off the edge after him. NO, NO, NO, NO!!! Internally I was screaming wildly but outwardly I was dead calm as I began to strip his heavy saddle and gear off. The bags I'd just put on only a few short, different hours before. My hands shook as I attempted to undo buckles and ties with my left-hand, ring finger tilting a definite unnatural list to the right.

Please be OK. Please be OK. Please be OK. Stay with me. Stay with me. Prayers sometimes come so strong you don't even realize you're making them. I willed him to take the breath that had gotten knocked out of him until he did take a big shuddering gasp, still while the shock rolled over him again. When a horse has become everything to you, closer than most people, the thought of that loss can paralyze.

It seemed like forever, but in reality, it was probably minutes as I rubbed his neck, my muddy hands smearing palm prints that almost dried as I touched him. I whispered in his ear "You're alright, I promise we're still going to make it." He began that awkward crawl horses do to lift themselves from the ground, front legs reaching until the back can scramble upright, tail slinging dirt in either direction.

Finally, I saw my finger, already doubling in size, joint to knuckle. I rested my head against his shoulder, willing the tears back in my eyes as I began the painstaking task of trying to tack a horse with one hand, the second hand barely usable. It was loose but it would hopefully get us to the top.

Consulting the map again we crept as steadily as we could towards the peak. Everything kept loosening and sliding because I couldn't get it quite tight enough until finally we reached the top and I took it all off again on solid soil. I changed clothes and broke a stick into three short pieces to craft a splint with vet wrap. It wasn't pretty but at least afforded support and prevented the slightest brush or knock that sent the pain coursing upwards again.

We meandered through the woods, searching for better ground until we popped out onto a reclaimed strip mine. Rob Roy stopping for grass all along the way, we finally came to a road. We'd passed this way on our way up to the terminus and I'd remembered seeing a house that was being renovated. Renovation meant people building on a work in progress.

Above the little green house was a small field with a rusted out hay shed shaped like an airplane hanger and what was once in a past life a fenced-in garden. Relieved, I ditched the gear into an outbuilding and set the horse up for the night. The night began to fall as I settled into the wooden floor of the shed with the leftover hay spread beneath my sleeping bag. I lay there staring into the darkness, wishing for some sort or any type of pain pill. All I had was an emergency bottle of Fireball. I'd packed Bute for the boy but nothing for myself.

The wind picked up into a fierce howl that blew the plastic shower curtain I'd set up as a door into my face. I set a boot on top but the wind just tossed it aside. Sleep proved near impossible in the face of the never-ending wind. It blew through the window and tunneled into my makeshift bed. I closed my eyes and dreamed of those I loved back home waiting for me.

The next morning my theories proved themselves true. I trudged down to the house; knocking on the door I discovered a father and son running power tools. The house smelled of sawdust and fresh-cut wood. I introduced myself, explained what I was doing and what had happened, lifting my splinted finger for emphasis. Deep in the mountains, there was no cell phone service and no way to reach out to the outside world.

"Go on down the road about a mile and a half and you'll hit the ex-sheriff of Randolph County. He'll help you out. Goes by Slugger. He'll have a phone you can use." I thanked them and started walking. I passed by the pipeline right of way, it's scarred surface marring the mountains. Further along, the pipeliners stood by an open gate, chatting around a big piece of machinery.

"Do you know where Slugger's house is?" They nodded and pointed further down the road from where we stood.

"Looks like it's gonna snow!" They called out after me. I looked up to the sky and the clouds were darkening the sky, a hazy gray smearing the clouds into the vastness. A lone cabin stood in a field; it's siding slowly rotting away. I circled it and peered through the windows, knocked on the door but no one responded. Another house, a larger farmhouse style stood out, further down the road. I aimed towards that one, white turkeys and geese swirling away and around me.

I knocked on the front door, still no answer. The knocks on the garage door created a staccato burst of barking from large sounding dogs. I stepped back quickly and moved onto the kitchen door. Nothing. I sat on the steps to wait for help to come, a human hand outstretched for another. A beggar, a panhandler with a busted finger, a stranger in a strange land with a rock for a pillow. It wasn't long of a wait before a large truck rumbled up, scattering the fowl in all directions. A teen girl jumped out of the passenger side and ran towards the door, a younger boy racing behind her, both skidding to a stop startled when they saw me on the stoop.

"Who are you?" A petite woman behind the wheel had rolled the window down and lobbed the question. This was always the best and the worst part for me, my private nature battling my needs.

"My name is Sarah. I'm camped up the road a ways. Some guys working on a house sent me your way to try to use the phone to call my support people." I wiggled my messed up hand in front of me, the sticks, and wraps bulging.

"Oh my goodness! You poor thing." She came scrambling out of the vehicle towards me and started unlocking the door. I started recounting the day before, the logging road, the mud, the fall, the snap, camping in the shed with the wind racing through. Her eyes widened a little, her skepticism starting to fade and melt.

We walked into the kitchen overflowing with food and snacks on every surface. My stomach rumbled. I didn't know what time it was and couldn't remember what I'd had for breakfast.

"The kids just got out of school, we'll be having dinner. Are you hungry?" Her politeness made me laugh inside, the noises my stomach was making could probably be heard in the next county over.

"Whatchu got in there?" A gruff voice trailed out of the adjoining room. A CB radio crackled behind his booming question.

"Some girl camping with her horse. Says her finger is broken." She called back to the disembodied voice, "I'm Debbie," she said, "That's my husband Paul."

"Do people call him Slugger?" I asked laughing.

"They sure do!" He called out from the other room.

"Then I'm in the right place!" I replied still laughing. And just like that, the ice was broken.

"Here's the phone." Debbie handed it to me and I pulled the slip of paper out with Jane Birdsong's number on it. Jane had been a huge helper when we had arrived at Weston to start our journey back home. I called and left a message and sat to wait while Debbie cooked.

"You can go on in the other room," she told me as she started pulling out supplies to make dinner, "I'll bring some Epsom salts and hot water to soak your hand."

I entered the TV room where Slugger sat on his throne. His stature dwarfed the space, the TV blared in the background as he turned the volume down and began his interrogation.

Debbie bustled in, her history as a nurse blindingly apparent. "Put your hand in this and let it soak until it gets cold. Paul, give her a moment's rest for God's sake."

I began undoing my bandage. I'd rewrapped it twice already, once before going to sleep and again in the morning, but the whole hand continued to swell and turn black and blue. It looked worse each time I took the wrap off.

"Whoa." Slugger was taken aback by the fact my hand was swollen up two times the size it should be. I sucked a breath in as I dunked it into the hot water, biting my lip to keep from yelping in front of the others.

"There you go. That'll help it a whole bunch." Debbie returned to the kitchen, the smells emanating from there sounded and smelled like heaven as they seeped into the adjoining room. The pain began to ease as the hot water did its trick.

I kept Slugger occupied with stories of the trail, highlights, and tough parts. He made sure to tell me he could sniff out a liar thanks to all his years on the police force. I wasn't trying to hide anything and the more we talked the more we both were put at ease. I told him of home, the man I was trying to get back to, and our love story. He told me of meeting Debbie in high school, that they had been together ever since. I'd always had a soft spot for real love stories like that.

As we talked, the snow that had been threatening earlier began falling in earnest. Big white flakes that stuck as soon as they landed, lulled me into complacency. The phone rang, jerking me out of my near doze.

"It's for you!" Debbie called out.

"Hello?" The precious voice on the other end was a familiar one. I gripped the phone to my ear in relief.

"Jane!" I hurriedly updated her on what had happened and what I needed. Grain was a constant struggle to carry along and to follow us further down the road. "...and a splint for my finger."

"What kind?" She asked.

"I dunno, I guess one of those metal ones?"

"Gotcha," she responded. "Be there in a bit." I carefully delivered the directions to get here, everything an eternity of winding roads from one place to the next.

"I've got a splint for you!" Slugger was helpful as I got off the phone. "Hold on," he hefted himself up from his chair. I slipped my hand back into the lukewarm water.

"Here you go," he tossed it on my lap. I laughed again; molded plastic and a broken plastic knife held together with some tape. Everything with Slugger was a tease and a wink and some cosmic joke.

"I didn't do too bad!" I held my twigs back up and he laughed back.

****

Jane had arrived after skidding on the worsening roads. We pored over the maps together, routing the way ahead. She'd brought two different splints to choose from and the rest of a bag of grain. Dinner had settled in my stomach and the Brady's had invited me to spend the night and take a shower. We drove to feed the old man and give him more water and grab some of the gear and a change of clothes.

Getting back, I washed the last of the mud off myself as the snow kept its steady pace. I called my man back home who was both patiently and not so patiently waiting for me, frustrated by the distance and the cause that had taken me away from him. Some nights the longing was so deep and fierce I fell asleep crying. This was one of those nights, but I had a bed and was as safe as I could be as I fell into the deepest and darkest sleep.

I stayed another day while the snow piled on top of itself again and again. I watched a herd of deer play in the drifts, boxing one another and leaping and sliding around one another. We watched the senior Bush's casket paraded down the street, all presidential regalia flying on the television. After my time in the roads and the wilderness, the moving images seemed so foreign and I could hardly keep my eyes away from them. I felt so far removed from the rest of civilization, both in distance and purpose.

The Brady's were taking their shut-in neighbor to the store preparing for the winter freeze in, the kids were off from school because of Bush, my finger felt incrementally better and it was time for me to head out.

"Be careful of the bears and bear hunters! Don't get in their way," Slugger yelled out the window as they headed out of their driveway. The season had just opened and the woods were to become full of hounds, guns, and trackers. He'd called out to them on the radio that morning warning them we were coming through and not to shoot blindly.

I geared up carefully; we'd decided it was best for me to take the access roads to get to Elk

Springs Resort who'd put us up on the way up. I marched and pushed through the snow like a bumbling bear. A forestry service vehicle passed by me, curiously.

"You must really like the snow," he shot out the window.

"Not really," I retorted with my usual red-headed sass.

He laughed, reiterated the cautions about bear season being dangerous, and kept on his route. We kept trudging along. I hated all the backtracking and covering ground I'd already been over, the access road was back where we'd seen the pipe-liners before. They'd cleared out with the coming of snow; it was the bear hunter's domain now.

I followed my little interactive map from the CSI pipeline group. It was a lifesaver that followed me via satellite live time. I was the blue dot moving increment by increment. Best of all it worked when I didn't have service, which was the majority of the remote and rugged state of West Virginia. I was confused with the little squiggly black lines of access roads which occasionally would dump me out unexpectedly or abruptly end.

I'd covered Rob Roy with the length of my unfolded sleeping bag to help keep him warm, saddle strapped on top. I pulled my phone back out of the ziplock baggie I'd been carrying it in. I'd been pulling it in and out non-stop; I couldn't figure out why our elevation was staying the same. We were supposed to be headed downhill into the valley; disgusted I wedged it back into my pocket. I was four layers deep at least in clothes. I fell in the snow; I trudged through streams hidden beneath it.

Again I stopped to check the map. My phone was gone and the bag was empty. My mind stopped as frozen as the landscape. It had taken us all a day to get to this lost point I was at and we were lucky if we had two hours of daylight left. I backtracked towards the last place I had remembered having it as everyone who has ever lost anything has done since time immemorial. I swept with my feet trying to clear and cover more ground.

I don't know how many times I passed over that same quarter-mile of ground, but finally unable to beat the darkness descending I began to set up camp in ten or so inches of snow. I tied Rob Roy to a tree as he continued pawing for any sort of greenery below. I crawled into my little one-man wormhole tent, shivering, and soaked. My sleeping bag had one little dry spot in the middle and I curled into a fetal position trying to garner any shred of warmth I could. It was the first night on the trip I thought I might not wake up in the morning.

But I did. My fingers were iced, the broken one still pulsing gently. I opened the tent made only slightly warmer with body heat than the air outside. Rob Roy had created a semi-circle of mud and snow around the tree I'd tied him to. I'd fed him his breakfast and started the camp stove boiling Ramen as best as I could to warm myself up internally.

I squatted in the snow remembering the dream the night before of an unknown man on an ATV vehicle finding my phone. I started packing and backtracked one last time to cover more ground in the hopes I would find it. How would I finish this without my maps and some sense of direction? I was truly shooting blindly now, stabbing in the direction of home.

I packed up again, still searching as I left. There was nothing I could do and my stomach twisted with the unknown of what was ahead. I tied a piece of string on a twig of a bush on the road I'd gone down and started up the hill on another road. It was a complicated rabbit's warren even though we'd entered at only one point. A pickup truck passed me and slowed when I waved. Startled by a lone woman and a seventeen hand high gray horse they rolled their window down.

"I lost my phone back there," I pointed down the hill to where we'd camped the night before, "It has all my maps on it." I gave them the cliff notes of why we were where we were, what we were doing, and what had happened. I mentioned Slugger's name.

"Yeah, we know him." They were brusque and eager to get on with the hunt.

"Can you let him know I'm OK? Can you tell him what happened?"

"Yeah, we will." And with that, they were off. "You're going the wrong way you know!" They shouted after me, "You should be going downhill."

I turned around again and back-tracked the way we came. We'd never get home at this rate. It was the beginning of December, would I make it in time for Christmas? We passed another bear hunter, the hounds already braying deep in the woods. Hot on the trail I hurriedly told them my predicament and continued. I missed my mark that night and stayed with some hospitable strangers. Almost missed it again another day. I was back to hand-drawn maps and colloquial directions, hard to follow at best.

None of the pipe-liners I passed were from in-state, even though Dominion touted all their job creation in their spiels. It was a local trucker who finally turned me around and I arrived at Elk Springs Resort in time to set up for the night, a hot dinner, and another call to Jane.

Jane came back with a metal detector, we hiked back to try to find the phone with no luck, slipping and sliding on refrozen ice it was a treacherous search. The detector went off just as it was dark with one headlight casting its glow between us. I cleared the snow but nothing could be seen or felt. Dejectedly I gave up. It was gone, all my pictures from the trip, all the contacts I had met along the way, my link to civilization in the desolation, my landline to home. It was sad this little thing of metal and glass meant so much to me, but I didn't know how to make my way without it.

But I would for almost two weeks. We were in Virginia counties away when the message from Slugger finally came in.

"I have your phone" was all it said.

OMIGODDDD!!!! A bear hunter had found it. I told him about the dream and that I would call him after dinner. We caught up, it had been almost two weeks since I had seen him last and I was two large counties away from home. Nine days until Christmas and I was pushing as hard as I could for the both of us. The Moore's who'd helped us and who's greatest hobby had become tracking us would eventually bring the phone back to us, lost ten days in the snow with no case, and working perfectly. We knew where we were, we were headed home.

****

We would make it home from West Virginia the day after Christmas. We would leave South on April 13th with two horses this time. Ultimately Rob Roy and I completed 1,000 miles. Nine lost toenails, five riding helmets, three pairs of boots, and a broken finger, we went the distance. Against all odds and obstacles. We completed the entire pipeline route through three states. The project would be announced as canceled July 5th, 2020 almost a year after our final return home.

Icebergs & Icelandic Horses in Greenland

BY KRYSTAL KELLY

The helicopter blades roared above us. My heart raced as the pilot pulled the lever, allowing us to take off and glide through the air. My view of the pilot was restricted. After all, this helicopter was first and foremost a parcel delivery carrier for the local mail, and secondly a transport for tourists. It made sense, considering upon our arrival we had only seen a pair of locals seated beside my husband and myself, and a handful of others. It didn't feel like the sort of place tourists frequented.

A huge smile stretched across my face as we hurtled through the sky. The view below of the peaks shadowing a bright blue ocean, peppered with icebergs, had my heart aflutter. I had always said that if I hadn't grown up to be a professional equestrian, my second career choice would have been a helicopter pilot.

Together with my husband, Christian, it was our first time sitting inside a helicopter. Even stuffed behind boxes and boxes of packages to be delivered to the Greenlandic people at our arrival destination, we were ecstatic for the opportunity.

After a thirty-minute flight, we arrived at our first stop: Qaqortoq. Qaqortoq is the largest city in South Greenland. Nuuk, the capital city, was a two-day's-long boat ride away, something we planned on visiting towards the end of our stay. For now, we were excited to explore our first Greenlandic "City."

We stepped off the helicopter and watched as the tractor drove to collect the parcels stacked inside the chopper. A man grabbed our two very small suitcases and threw them inside the back of the trailer before revving his tractor into gear. We walked to the small building, which was assumed to be the airport terminal for helicopters, and watched as the man driving the tractor tossed our bags into the small hole in the wall. Our bags landed onto the tiniest conveyer belt we'd ever seen. As we were the only two people in the building we grabbed our two small carry-ons and exited into the real world.

We had pre-arranged an apartment for the night all to ourselves. From the photos, the adorable, brightly-painted red house seemed to be nestled on the mountainside, with a view overlooking the port, helipad, and city. We followed our instructions and walked on the road leading to the house that would be ours for the night. The road was without cars, however, cars could be seen parked outside every house.

We arrived at our stay and were met with a large set of stairs. I braced myself for the big climb and eventually arrived at one of the most spectacular views. The photos did not do it justice.

Qaqortoq was in a word: adorable. The colorfully painted houses were bright and vivid. Purples, blues, reds, greens, pinks, and yellows dotted the mountainside across from us. We were perched on one of the outer edges of a "bowl" it seemed, with the boat harbor and helipad down below in the center of the town.

I took in a deep breath, feeling like I'd been transported into another world. And this was only the first day! I couldn't wait to see what the following three weeks would bring.

****

My husband and I had caught a flight from Iceland to Narsarsuaq in the South of Greenland. The flight wasn't long, it was a small plane with mostly danish backpackers wearing matching North Face hiking pants and jackets.

My husband and I didn't fit in with the crowd, our tall Ariat riding boots were our biggest giveaway. I was sporting my Equestrian Adventuresses hoodie, praying that my Californian lack of ability to handle the cold would survive one of the coldest places on Earth. I took solace in the fact that it was early August, still summer in my mind, and I hoped that that would be enough for light winter wear.

Christian, on the other hand, is from Eastern Germany. Stepping off the plane he began stripping his layers off and was soon down to just a single light jacket. Later, I would learn from our other Eastern German guests joining our group on this horse riding expedition, this was considered "hot" weather. (During the riding we luckily experienced some of the warmest weather in Greenland and the horses began to sweat! I personally never stripped my layers down much but then again I was the only person in this riding group from a warm climate...)

Christian and I were in Greenland on a mission. Not only did we want to experience Greenland from horseback and learn as much as we could about the culture, food, traditions, and people, but we had another, more grand quest at stake. We were there to make a documentary film for the Equestrian Adventuresses Prime Series on Amazon.

*You can watch the show on Amazon Prime, the Equus Film Channel or simply visit our website:
www.EquestrianAdventuresses.com

And the star of the show was going to be the woman behind the only horse riding operation in all of Greenland run by locals. Her name was Aajunnguaq—"Aaju," for short—and I was excited to meet her.

When I set out to create a Documentary Series for Equestrian Adventuresses, my mission was simple: To inspire and empower women to achieve their horse & travel dreams by sharing the stories of amazing women in the equine industry. I knew that Aaju was the perfect candidate to educate outsiders on the beauty of her country. And what better way to see the beauty than on the back of a horse with a group of Adventuresses!

Masaatsiaq, her husband, and Aaju started the horse riding tours about 4 years ago. They already had horses because they are sheep farmers and use the Icelandic horses to gather their 300+ sheep from the mountains before winter comes. Masaatsiaq was a silent man, but a very hard worker. He greeted us warmly with his boat and took us across the bay to his quaint farm. Although his skin was dark, he had bright blue eyes. He was short but handsome. I wondered how beautiful Aaju must be to have landed a man like that.

The first time I saw Aaju, she was exactly what I expected. Masaatsiaq had picked our group up in his small boat and carried us to the bay—complete with an iceberg—where the sheep and horse farm is located. Aaju was there to greet us, and to help Masaatsiaq steer the boat close to the rocks.

"Hi!" She waved to us before grabbing onto the boat as she balanced atop the deadly rocks. She steadied the boat as we, one-by-one, climbed quickly onto the rocks. Her two small children danced around the truck parked at the top of the hill on the shore. She then launched herself onto the boat while her husband carried on in the driver's seat, grabbed the first and largest bag—belonging to one of the ladies accompanying us on this adventure—and handed it to Christian so he could pass it onto another girl waiting at the top of the rocks. We formed a line and quickly and efficiently removed all bags from the boat so Masaatsiaq could push off and anchor inside the bay.

Aaju had fair skin with dark eyes and hair. She was very slender and the type of woman that could easily have been the next Heidi Klum. She looked like she should be on the cover of Vogue, not out here in the middle of nowhere loading bags. I secretly wondered what the hell was in the water to make the people this damn pretty. Ok, so I hadn't exactly met many Greenlandic people in my travels, but it seemed the combination of Scandinavian and Inuit blood created some kind of miracle combination.

"Nice to meet you," Aaju introduced herself as she finally made it back onto shore. She directed us to the house where we would be staying for the next week as she loaded our things into the back of her pickup truck. "I'll meet you there!" She called as she scooted her small children away from the truck.

****

The horses we were given were very healthy and rugged. They were all Icelandic horses and spent most of their days roaming the mountains. Horses are not common in Greenland, however, in the South there are a lot of sheep farms. Since the sheep spend the summers roaming the mountains freely, the horses are only used one month out of the year to help herd the sheep before winter. The sheep would then spend the frozen winter months kept inside a large barn. Although I didn't like the thought of being trapped indoors for months on end, the thought of spending the harsh Greenlandic winters outside in the cold sounded even less appealing.

Aaju and Masaatsiaq's horses had been leading tourist groups for a few years now and were used to having a summer job apart from herding sheep. This means they had less time in the mountains in the summer but spent the majority of the year (about 8 months) roaming wild in the mountains. Due to this, they were extremely sure-footed.

Their Icelandic "tolt" (their extra gait) is very comfortable to ride and I enjoyed sitting on a sofa-like horse for the week. I adored my little Icelandic horse, Picolo. Picolo was convinced that he was Seabiscuit and loved nothing more than to try and race the others. Picolo and I spent most of the week leading the group with Masaatsiaq somewhere behind us leading the others. Luckily for me, there weren't many trails or places to get lost and so I could ride with loose reins and allow my mighty pony the chance to pick and choose his path.

The other ladies joining us on the group were matched with their ideal horses for the ride. They too fell in love with their calm, easy-going Icelandic horses. Christian got a horse named Charlie, who we were told would be the best match for him to film from.

Christian and Charlie developed a funny relationship during our week-long riding adventure. Because the horses are sheep herding horses first and tour horses second, Charlie didn't have a problem with Christian dismounting randomly to film something. Charlie would simply stand by himself and take a quiet nap in the sunshine while Christian ran up the stones to get the best shot.

Eventually, Christian would return to Charlie and mount up and canter to catch up with the rest of us. Only once or twice did Charlie decide to leave Christian on his own to catch up on foot.

Greenland is an extreme place where—in my mind at least—people aren't supposed to survive. Yet people have been living in Greenland since the Vikings first discovered it over 1,000 years ago. The Vikings were in Greenland for about 400 years but they eventually disappeared. The Greenlandic Inuit tribes, however, thrived. They were better adapted to the extreme nature and toughness of Greenland. They fished, hunted for whales and seals, and dressed in seal and polar bear fur to stay warm.

Nowadays, the climate is warming up and we witnessed many icebergs breaking off of the nearby glaciers and floating in the fjords. Seeing the glaciers and icebergs was an out-of-body experience for me. I never would have imagined seeing such a thing growing up in California! We even rode our horses around some of the icebergs that had washed up on one of the beaches and enjoyed a good canter. Sometimes you could hear the icebergs cracking and breaking during our ride, but our horses were used to the loud booming sound of icebergs and didn't even bat an eye.

Masaatsiaq was our guide and was in charge of taking us to new destinations each day on horseback. Aaju was in charge of cooking our dinner and arranging and organizing everything. Aaju was very eager to share stories about her life in Greenland and was open and honest about sharing the life and culture of her people.

"In America," I said to her one evening, "we have Earthquake drills in school in California for the kids. And when I moved to Oklahoma, we had to learn tornado drills instead of Earthquake drills. Do you have any sort of drills for the kids at school here?" I asked.

Aaju pursed her lips in thought. "Well, we have polar bears obviously," she said.

"Oh! And what do they teach you in school?"

"Well," she said animately, her hands waving as she spoke, "They taught us that if a polar bear sees you, first they do that," she rocked back and raised her two arms as if they were bear paws. "They stand on their hinds with their paws in the air like that. And then they do that," she swiped her right paw at an imaginary school kid.

"And then?" I was on the edge of my seat.

"And then you're dead." She shrugged.

"What?! That's what they teach you in school?" I was in disbelief.

"Well, no one will survive a polar bear attack..."

"Have you ever seen a polar bear?" I asked, completely lost in her words now.

"A few times polar bears have come. They don't belong here. They belong in the north and usually live on the glacier."

The Glacier in Greenland makes up over 80% of the entire landmass. This ice sheet is the second largest ice mass in the world—with Antarctica being the first largest.

Aaju continued, "the polar bears float down to South Greenland on icebergs. They are very good swimmers and one time there was a polar bear swimming not too far from here. Masaatsiaq and the other sheep farmers all are on polar bear watch in the winter so if there is a sighting we call and warn everyone in all the villages. Then the men try to find the polar bear and keep an eye on it that it doesn't go near the people or try to eat the sheep.

So, one time when this polar bear was seen swimming in the bay Masaatsiaq took me in the boat with him and we went with the other farmers and followed the bear while it swam across the bay. I got right next to the bear. It was making heavy breathing noises from swimming and its paws were in the water and his muscles were moving... Polar Bears are so big and powerful. They are so scary. Even with the bear in the water, I was so afraid."

The next day we rode out. Today we were riding to another glacier and spent several hours climbing up the mountains to the viewpoint. We stopped for a picnic lunch, unsaddled the horses, and sat in silence as we stared in awe at the glacier in the distance. The icebergs floated calmly around the glacier. Never in a million years, having grown up in sunny California did I ever think I would witness icebergs breaking off a glacier. The rumble of the ice as it cracked and fell into the water echoed in the valley and I felt the hair on the back of my neck stand.

It didn't take me long to realize how much work both Masaatsiaq and Aaju put into their sheep farm and the horse riding tours. During the day Masaatsiaq would take us on long adventurous rides and in the evening he was on his tractor baling hay. He needs to bale the hay for the sheep to survive the long winter months inside the barn. It didn't get dark at night and Masaatsiaq took advantage of the light as much as possible, baling the hay until 10 pm.

Aaju was also very busy. With two small children to care for and look after and a husband and 6 guests to feed, she was often in the kitchen preparing something or other. She also came to help us prepare the horses and it was clear that her knowledge and love of her animals ran deep. She affectionately greeted the horses upon sight and told us the story of how she and Masaatsiaq came into possession of every one of the horses.

"Charlie was one of our first horses," she explained as she patted him on the neck. "We traded him for some recyclable bottles." We laughed. "No, it's true! In Greenland, bottles are very expensive. Well, most goods are very expensive. We don't grow our goods or products, so apart from fish and our sheep, everything has to be imported. And I mean EVERYTHING!"

I thought about my visit to a local grocery store while staying the night in Qaqortoq. The price tags on the foods were absolutely absurd. I had paid nearly $10 just for a chocolate bar, only to convert the money later and realize my mistake. After that, we were careful about what we spent our money on.

"Actually," Aaju confessed, "the Government stipends us for the sheep because its cheaper to import sheep-meat and wool from New Zealand than it is to sell our sheep to the markets. We sheep farmers make a living with our sheep funding from the government and without this money, we would surely go out of business."

I was taken aback by this new information. I knew that Denmark owned Greenland and that they transported goods to this large island, but I couldn't quite figure out how this desolate place survived.

In Qaqortoq, our host, a very friendly insurance salesman, had given Christian and I a tour of his city. Qaqortoq was the largest city in the South of Greenland, holding 3,500 people in total. They had 2 kilometers of road in total, but EVERYONE had a car. Some families even had two cars! Our host had not hesitated to invite the two of us into his car so he could drive us around on a sightseeing tour of the city. He took us to nearly every house and building, regaling us with stories of the building's history and his life growing up in this city.

That experience had struck me and it was interesting to hear from Aaju what it was like to live the life of a Greenlandic sheep farmer. Sheep farming only existed in the south, where the weather was supposed to be "better." Nuuk, the capital city towards the middle of this large glacial landmass was known for its port. The harbor made it ideal for trading. Especially the main export item: fish.

We saddled our horses and set off on another spectacular ride. I was completely in awe of the scenery. The mountains were formidable-looking and the land was desolate. I wondered what the sheep and horses were eating because I had a hard time finding much grass.

Charlie was an old gentleman and Christian had a great time with him. Charlie didn't tolt, however, so unfortunately Christian's ride wasn't quite as comfortable as the rest of us.

Meanwhile, Picolo and I enjoyed hanging out in front and sometimes swapped places with Masaatsiaq as the leader. Unless a good canter was coming, in which case Picolo and I loved to hang out in the back and let the others scoot ahead before dropping the reins and flying across the land at heart-pounding speed to catch up. It was my first time to ever ride on Icelandic horses and I was sold.

"I'm going to have to bring my mom on a horse riding holiday to Iceland and buy her an Icelandic horse," I told Christian. Christian made a face as Charlie's bouncy trot-like-tolt continuously shook him out of the saddle.

"I don't know, I can't rise to Charlie's trot but I also can't sit it," he laughed. "Both are equally uncomfortable." He squeezed Charlie into a slow canter, a sense of relief washing over his face. "The canter is lovely though!" Picolo's speedy trot was equal to Charlie's canter and we had no problem keeping the same pace with the others.

We rode high into the mountains. There were a few times where the sheer drops on the side caused my heart to race. I entrusted my sure-footed horse to keep me safe as we wound our way up the tiny trail.

"We are trying a new way," Masaatsiaq confessed as he double-backed onto a different slope. I felt like Indiana Jones, except there weren't any bushes to wack through with a machete.

As we neared the top, our horses were able to catch their breath. A ledge appeared and Masaatsiaq dismounted. "Here we can eat our picnic lunches," he called to us as he began unsaddling his horse. We followed suit and tied our horses to the various stones and shrubs.

The view overlooked a large glacier and I was overwhelmed by the sight. Thousands of icebergs floated silently in the bright blue water. This was the closest I had ever been to a glacier and our view from the mountain top couldn't have been more perfect.

Our group of ragtag riders had spent the entire ride chatting away happily, but at this moment we each found a place to sit in silence and watch the surroundings. Lost in our thoughts we nibbled on our sandwiches. Christian and I sat side by side, appreciating the moment. My eyes tried to memorize every iceberg, the sights and smells of the horses resting beside us, and the impressive ice sheet shadowing us all.

I envisioned what it must be like to cross that ice sheet. If the Greenlandic ice sheet would melt, the ocean level would rise about 6 meters. If you were to try and cross from the West to the East of Greenland you'd have several mountains to cross, polar bears to fend off, and extreme temperatures to battle. The journey from West to

East would take approximately 36 days (if you were able to make it at all that is.)

It seemed surreal to me to have so much ice gathered in one place. My eyes blinked, still not fully believing the view that stretched out before me. I understood, in that pristine place, why Masaatsiaq and Aaju loved their home so much. Nowhere else on Earth had felt so wild, free, and untouched as this place did to me.

After an hour of rest enjoying the peacefulness, we saddled our horses and continued our ride to our next destination. Spending hours in the saddle in this wild and desolate place on Picolo gave me time to reflect and rejuvenate. I felt lucky to experience this place and to have been able to share it with my husband and the other adventuresses who had joined me on this adventure.

During our stay, Aaju confessed to me her dream to take over the riding tours. "I'm just waiting for the kids to grow, then it will be my turn," she said. I knew that I would have to return one day soon to coach her. In fact, that was one of the reasons I had become an FEI Level II Showjumping coach during my travels. My talent for horses needed to be shared with others such as Aaju.

I can't tell you how many times I met women with a love for horses and a lack of access to good riding instruction. Especially when the only instructors around were macho men that weren't too keen on allowing women to ride. This made my mission all the more ingrained in my heart and I focused my career on educating men in various cultures to allow women to ride and empowering women to get in the saddle! I silently prayed that the Equestrian Adventuresses documentary series would help inspire more women to get in the saddle and prove to men that riding isn't just for the boys.

"In Greenland," she continued, "there aren't any people to teach you things like horsemanship or how to ride correctly or how to train horses to be ridden more naturally. It's mostly men riding horses because the men herd the sheep while the women stay home and cook. The women have to have the meals ready for when the men return with the sheep." I pursed my lips. I had seen this before many times. "I like to be outside though," she said as she gazed into the distance. "I like to fix the fences, I like to care for the sheep."

I felt my heart reaching out to her and I knew that she would get her chance to ride. "Have you ever ridden?" I asked.

"Yes, a little." She shared stories about her beloved gray mare roaming in the mountains. She shared a special bond with that mare and had even sat on her without any saddle or halter on her face. "It was very fast that I fell in love with horses," Aaju smiled, a twinkle in her eye.

I recognized that look all too well. I knew how addictive horses were from a lifetime of experience. I knew that she had been bitten by the "horse-bug," for which there was no cure. I was confident that Aaju would go on to be the only Greenlandic woman leading horse riding expeditions and nothing made me feel prouder.

When I spoke to her husband, Masaatsiaq, he confirmed the same vision. "I was a bit shocked when I saw it was only ladies coming to ride horses. I didn't mind so many ladies of course," he laughed. "But I think Aaju will take over the horse riding tours. I will help teach her to ride."

It was amazing to witness a couple as progressive as Aaju and Masaatsiaq. Not only were they trailblazers on the trails, but they were trailblazers in business and in life too.

The horse riding tour was an amazing experience, something I could only have dreamed about as a child. Because of their hard work and dedication to making the vision a reality, now everyone with riding experience can come and take part in this trip.

And to think that four years ago it was nothing more than an idea is surely enough in itself to inspire others in similar countries with similar ideas to also trail blaze new riding opportunities.

And I can't wait to be the one to see it!

****

Christian and I sat on the smooth rocks perched beside the shore. The gentle flow of the waves splashing on the rocks was a soothing sound. I rested my head on his shoulder as we held hands and admired the view. The large iceberg that had called the bay beside Aaju and Masaatsiaq's farm home, was the frame for our mental canvas. In the corner of the picturesque setting was the sight of the horses grazing happily on the hillside.

My eyes absorbed the beautiful blue colors that danced inside the iceberg and I sighed a deep breath of relief. Christian shot me a warm smile as he pulled me into a tight hug. In all my years of globetrotting, I never thought I would have come so far. I thought back to my past travels working with horses in places like Romania, Italy and Egypt. Although the memories were mostly pleasant ones, I knew that this moment would be hard to beat.

Staring at the view of Greenland, as I sat beside my husband—my fellow riding and traveling companion—I felt as if the world had opened up a new realm of possibilities. There was something special about sharing magical moments like these with someone. After years spent wandering the planet as a solo traveler, it felt nice to have finally found my teammate.

I smiled back at him, a slight grin forming in the corner of my mouth. I didn't know where we would end up next, or how we would get there. I simply knew this wouldn't be our last equestrian adventure together. And I was excited to see what the future horizon would bring.

Thank You For Reading!

Dear Reader,

I hope you enjoyed this 4th installment in the Equestrian Adventuresses Book Series. I have to tell you, I really love stories from adventuresses just like you. If you crave more stories like these, fear not, we will be back in Book 5 of the Series. As an author, I love feedback. I have received many messages from readers thanking me for this series for inspiring them to travel on horseback and take a chance.

You are the reason I will keep seeking stories from amazing Equestrian Adventuresses. Please let us know what you liked, loved and even what you hated. I'd love to hear from you. You can email me at www.equestrianadventuresses.com or post in our Facebook Group.

I need to ask a favor. If your so inclined, I'd love it if you would post a review on Amazon. Loved it, hated it—I'd just like to hear your feedback. Reviews can be tough to come by these days, and you, the reader, have the power to make or break a book. If you have the time, here's a link to my

author page, along with all my books on amazon:
www.amazon.com/author/krystal-kelly

Thank you so much for reading *Have Breeches Will Travel* and for spending time with me. I look forward to many more adventures together in the future!

In Gratitude,
Krystal Kelly
Equestrian Adventuresses Founder

About Equestrian Adventuresses

Equestrian Adventuresses was founded in 2019 as a community for women who love horses, travel and adventure. Our mission is to empower people around the world to follow their dreams and have amazing adventures on horseback. You can listen to more inspirational stories from real women's travels on horseback on the podcast show available on iTunes, Spotify, Stitcher and more.

You can also find a variety of travel documentaries on the Youtube Channel: www.youtube.com/c/equestrianadventuresses as well as read short stories and find helpful resources on the website: www.equestrianadventuresses.com

Join the community and check out the Facebook Group: EquestrianAdventuresses

Other Books By Equestrian Adventuresses:

EQUESTRIAN ADVENTURESSES SERIES

Book 1: Saddles and Sisterhood
Book 2: Going the Distance
Book 3: Leg Up
Book 4: Have Breeches Will Travel

TRAVEL GUIDE FOR EQUESTRIANS SERIES

Best in 2020 World Travel Guide
Best in 2020 USA Travel Guide
2021 Job Book - How to Work Abroad with Horses
Horse Riding in Every Country Catalog: A Catalog of 400+ Riding Opportunities in Over 180+ Countries

*Download your FREE E-Book here:
www.EquestrianAdventuresses.com

Coming Soon!
Equestrian Adventuresses Book 5

Dreaming of Traveling the World on Horseback but Don't Know Where to Start?

Introducing the **Equestrian Adventuresses Online Courses,** the first ever online home-study courses that gives you the necessary confidence and skills to become an equestrian adventuress.

What you'll learn:
- How to Speak the Horse Language in ANY country
- How to be more confident on the ground and in the saddle with horses
- How to travel solo confidently
- Develop a "Sticky Butt" in the saddle
- How to gain your horse's trust and build their confidence
- Mastering your own body language
- What is "Energy" and how does it influence your horse
- How to stay safe while traveling as a solo woman
- How to read situations

- Effective strategies to turn your goals, ideas & dreams into ACTIONABLE PLANS
- And much, much more!

For more information check out the Equestrian Adventuresses Online Courses Here:

www.EquestrianAdventuresses.com

About the Author
Amanda Champert

Amanda Champert, at an unknown age was given a Fisher Price camera. Along the way she also picked up an uncontrollable desire to travel, living and growing up in many different countries and now officially a travel addict and building up an impressive photo library, traveling across Morocco; where she discovered the most fascinating culture. The country where she fell in love with riding Barb-Arab stallions four years ago; cantering across the desert, oasis and mountainscapes. She journeyed for an entire month along the Moroccan-Algerian border and hopes to continue photographing her adventures.

https://amandachampert.wixsite.com/portfolio

About the Author
Maria Bros Pont

Maria Bros Pont was born in Sant Martí de Riucorb (Spain) in 1992. She graduated in veterinary medicine in 2015 for Autonomous University of Barcelona. Since then she has combined her two great passions, horses and traveling. She specialized in equine veterinary medicine and did two internships in France and United States. She is a certified equine acupuncturist from IVAS and is finishing her Masters Degree in Equine Sports Medicine for University of Cordoba. She currently works in her own ambulatory practice between Spain and France, and combines it with volunteers, either as a rider or a veterinarian.

www.instagram.com/maria.bros.veterinaria/

About the Author
Sarah Murphy

Sarah Murphy has been involved in the horse industry for over twenty years. Some of her experiences include teaching, breeding, barn managing, working the backside of a thoroughbred race training track and long riding. Most recently she completed a 1,000 mile ride in reaction to a proposed pipeline project. This ride earned her admittance into the Long Riders Guild, an international organization for long distance riders. She also completed a shorter 300 mile ride against mountaintop removal a decade prior.

www.acponhorseback.tumblr.com

About the Author
Krystal Kelly

Krystal Kelly is founder of Equestrian Adventuresses and an avid traveler on a quest to visit every country in the world. She left her home in California at the age of 21 to work abroad with top show jumping horses. She has since worked in over 20 countries with horses including Egypt, India, Romania, and many others. In 2016 she met her husband in Azerbaijan while driving a crappy car from England to Mongolia and back. Her love of adventurous travel has led her to the farthest corners of the Earth to film for the Equestrian Adventuresses Documentary series, available on Amazon Prime, the Equus Film Channel and the Equestrian Adventuresses website. She enjoys bringing her husband along for the ride to capture the beauty on film.

www.equestrianadventuresses.com

**ENJOYED THIS BOOK?
PLEASE LEAVE A REVIEW
ON AMAZON!**